HAWTHORNE'S
HISTORICAL ALLEGORY

KENNIKAT PRESS

NATIONAL UNIVERSITY PUBLICATIONS

SERIES ON LITERARY CRITICISM

General Editor

EUGENE GOODHEART

Professor of Literature, Massachusetts Institute of Technology

John E. Becker

HAWTHORNE'S

NATIONAL UNIVERSITY
PUBLICATIONS

HISTORICAL ALLEGORY

An Examination of the American Conscience

KENNIKAT PRESS
Port Washington, N. Y. ● London

Library of Congress Catalog Card Number: 78-139350
ISBN 0-8046-9002-2

Manufactured in the United States of America

Published by
Kennikat Press, Inc.
Port Washington, N.Y./London

For Claire

Contents

HAWTHORNE'S
HISTORICAL ALLEGORY

Introduction

Hawthorne is often embarrassing to his critics. Many of his characters are compelling and resonant; but, on reflection, they turn out to lack the three-dimensional quality which good characterization would seem to require. His imagery tends to shy away from symbols with potentially infinite but implicit meaning. He favors a more explicit, intellectually controlled relationship between symbol and significance. His structural principles are disconcertingly simple: a procession, a simple series of encounters, even mere enumeration or cataloguing of objects and people. Hawthorne, besides, plays maddeningly between the historical world and another world of dreamed history, thereby disarming criticism of the tools it uses on realistic fiction. All in all, it is difficult to know how to have him, the felt success of his stories is so frequently at odds with the canons not only of the realistic, but also of the symbolistic novel.

Many have called him an allegorist; it is almost inevitable that prolonged contact with Hawthorne should suggest this critical category. But he is certainly not an allegorist in the traditional sense. He seems too skeptical, too unsure; he rejects the systems of thought he knew, both scientific and religious. Still, apart from history, Hawthorne's favorite literature, man and boy, was the writing of Bunyan and Spenser. Besides, he seemed to take the spiritual problems of his Puritan forbearers, inveterate allegorists, more seriously than any other prominent writer of his time. One feels the continuity between him and them.

The Puritans exercised their allegorical bent chiefly in the interpretation of history, and history is also Hawthorne's favorite arena of fictional speculation. This conjunction of history and

3

allegory suggests the possibility that some form of biblical typology, that is, the interpretation of historical events in terms of past events and future expectations rather than abstract concepts, is the literary characteristic which binds Hawthorne to his Puritan ancestors and distinguishes him from the traditional allegorists. Erich Auerbach's investigation of typology, or *figura*, terminates with Dante.[1] But a recent German critic, Ursula Brumm, has carried the study on through the Dutch Protestant theologians and across the sea to America.[2] Miss Brumm's thesis is that typology is the distinguishing characteristic of the Puritan literary tradition in America, and this study was initially undertaken to question it. Miss Brumm recognizes that by the time of Jonathan Edwards the concept of typology had been virtually emptied of its historical reference. The close analysis of Hawthorne that I have tried to present in this study has forced me to the conclusion that typology is not as relevant to his technical apparatus as a more traditional form of allegory.

We are left, then, with allegory as still the closest approximation to a correct critical designation of Hawthorne's best work. It is not necessary, however, merely to be content with the term *allegory* as a negative approximation. Some recent writing on allegory has made it possible to flex the rigid boundaries of the term. Edwin Honig's *Dark Conceit* shows how allegory has endured as a literary form through radical shifts in the history of culture and ideas.[3] Angus Fletcher's *Allegory: The Theory of a Symbolic Mode* approaches allegory by isolating its techniques.[4] When one looks at Hawthorne through the lenses these authors have ground, the particularities of his writing, its violations of realism, its serial structures, even its ambiguity, leap to the eye as a single shape. They are no longer a catalogue of techniques but the coherent form of allegory reshaped and redefined.

One must abandon, then, the futile attempt to apply the criteria of realistic or symbolistic fiction to Hawthorne. But one must also let loose of a false criterion for allegory: that it is the fictional tricking-out of an independent structure of ideas, a structure which can be paraphrased without benefit of its accompanying fiction. Hawthorne demands, allegory demands, that we re-read him with an eye to the possibility that, using allegory's traditional techniques, he re-structured the overall formula. At root, this is merely the application of an old insight: every artist re-shapes the form in which he works; artist and form define each other. The critic's responsibility is the one he has usually assumed: to perceive and present the individuality of his author in terms of the literary tradition within which he has written and which he necessarily modifies. It is only that in our time allegory has seemed too unpliable to too many critics.

This present study is, consequently, an effort to define Hawthorne in terms of allegory and to show how Hawthorne reformulated allegory—even while he denied it the honor it still deserved. His "blasted allegories" have turned out to be, it seems to me, his best work. Chapter I is an examination of some of Hawthorne's historical tales, both to demonstrate the pervasive presence of allegorical techniques, and to make preliminary observations about the way Hawthorne shapes them into his own history-oriented allegory. Interpretation is only incidental in this first chapter. Chapters II and III on "The Custom-House" and *The Scarlet Letter* are a full-scale effort to prove that this, Hawthorne's climactic allegorical effort, is a unified allegory whose use of allegorical techniques is both traditional and original. The important facts here are Hawthorne's special relationship to both his readers and his story and an allegorical characterization which paradoxically turns its necessary reduction of the dimensions of personality into a form of superior psychological realism. Chapter IV is a summing up: a profile of Hawthorne's allegory and a sketch with commentary of some of the efforts of critics to get at the historical dimension of Hawthorne's work.

I have not here attempted a complete re-reading of Hawthorne. I have been interested, rather, in defending a basic insight, shared with many critics, that Hawthorne, in his best work, is an allegorist. I have gone beyond most of the critics in attempting to show that one cannot call Hawthorne an allegorist without entering into a discussion of his adaptation of the form. What has been lacking, and what Honig and Fletcher have supplied, is a more flexible sense of allegory. Alerted by their insights, I hope that I have been able to appreciate both the novelty of Hawthorne's contributions to allegory as well as the bond of union which kept him a faithful allegorist as he injected new vitality into an ancient and honorable literary tradition.

NOTES

[1] "Figura," *Scenes from the Drama of European Literature* (New York: Meridian Books, Inc., 1959), pp. 11-76.

[2] *American Thought and Religious Typology,* translated by John Hoaglund (New Brunswick, New Jersey: Rutgers University Press, 1970).

[3] ("A Galaxy Book," paper; New York: Oxford University Press, 1966).

[4] (Ithaca, New York: Cornell University Press, 1964).

Some Historical Tales

My Kinsman, Major Molineux

Critics are virtually unanimous in calling "My Kinsman, Major Molineux" an allegory.[1] The dream quality of the story has been noted as an allegorical technique. But more can be said, especially about the way in which dream fits into the seemingly alien context of the introductory historical essay.

Hawthorne opens his story of Robin with a paragraph of historical background. The prose is complex, circumlocutious, subtly balanced:

> After the kings of Great Britain had assumed the right of appointing the colonial governors, the measures of the latter seldom met with the ready and general approbation which had been paid to those of their predecessors, under the original charters. The people looked with most jealous scrutiny to the exercise of power which did not emanate from themselves, and they usually rewarded their rulers with slender gratitude for the compliances by which, in softening their instructions from beyond the sea, they had incurred the reprehension of those who gave them. (1209)[2]

The style is formal and abstract. Hawthorne trades the realistic plunge into the middle of his story for a detached and meditative return into time. The question is why should an allegory, which belongs to the literary tradition of Dante, Spenser, and Bunyan, be set back in time, rather than set off in a fictional world such as those great authors were forced to create. Hawthorne, after all, is not interested in history as history. He tries, rather, "to

7

transmute an historical phenomenon into an elemental condition of existence."[3]

There are, for our purposes, at least three reasons for Hawthorne's use of history: one rhetorical, flowing from the cast of mind of his audience; another more properly esthetic, flowing from the particular form of allegory which Hawthorne wished to write; and a third which we may call mythic, flowing from the interest Hawthorne has in interpreting America to itself by means of its past. This last we shall come to in connection with allegory and dream. For the moment we will consider the first two.

The European audiences of the great allegorists were willing to accept the validity of comments on life made within the setting of a fictitious narrative world. Writers within the old-world tradition of literary culture could confidently employ overtly literary structures for their reflections on existence: dream, romance, allegory, travel narrative. Hawthorne, on the other hand, "begged for the license in creating atmosphere which the European reader took for granted, but which the too literal-minded American public denied."[4]

But Hawthorne did more than beg for the license to create atmosphere. The prevailing Scottish common sense philosophy had set up a dichotomy between fact and fiction, reality and imagination, actuality and possibility. History obviously belonged to the preferred category of actuality, fact, reality.[5] Hawthorne, therefore, from the beginning, respected the world with which he was trying to open an intercourse, by appealing to its confidence in the value of history. The stricture against imagination was lulled by the illusion of history.

But the meditative consideration of the historical past, characteristic of Hawthorne, serves another more specifically formal purpose. We will see this more clearly in *The Scarlet Letter;* but Hawthorne's use of history here will serve to prepare for his more pervasive use of it there. The essay-like introduction to "My Kinsman, Major Molineux" places Hawthorne clearly before the reader's consciousness and induces him to stand, with the author, outside the story. Hawthorne does not want us to become immersed in the realities of novelistic fiction. He wants us to see, with detachment, the meaning of Robin's action and the action of the citizens. Consequently, though we see and accept the laughter which pervades and climaxes the story as meaningful within the political and psychological allegory of the story, we do not join in that laughter. We stand aside with Hawthorne and maintain a realistic perspective that allows us to say, with Hawthorne, that no matter how appropriate the laughter may be within the story itself, it is a senseless and cruel thing:

> On they went, like fiends that throng in mockery around some dead potentate, mighty no more, but majestic still in his agony. On they went, in counterfeited pomp, in senseless uproar, in frenzied merriment, trampling all on an old man's heart. On swept the tumult, and left a silent street behind. (1222)

In other words, Hawthorne reasserts at the end of the story, the detached perspective which he had established in his historical essay at the beginning. The reader of Hawthorne's allegory must not let himself become absorbed into the story. He must remain apart, ready for the interpretative comment of an author who prefers to stand aside and meditate.

It is necessary, then, to note Hawthorne's feint in the direction of history, if we are to read rightly the non-realistic creations of his allegorical imagination. It is a midsummer night, a hundred historical years ago, into which the ferryman carries Robin; but it is also a midsummer night's dream. It is, moreover, an allegorical dream, created within the tradition of such dreams. The anonymous ferryman is the figure of Charon. Robert Lowell makes this explicit in his dramatization of the story. The emphasis on the fare is another facet of the dream-visit to the underworld which Lowell makes explicit. We think of the sad fate of the dead stranded for all eternity on the near shore of eternity for lack of the proper fare. Finally Lowell's ferryman calls Boston the city of the dead:

> *Ferryman*
> Legs go round in circles here.
> This is the city of the dead.
> *Robin*
> What's that?
> *Ferryman*
> I said this city's Boston,
> No one begs here. Are you deaf?[6]

Hawthorne has brought us into the thinly masked underworld, familiar to us from Homer, Virgil, Dante, and the rest of Western literary history, in spite of the fact that he seems to be placing us securely on the surface of colonial America.

The dream, in real life, is an expression of the personality which it only becomes important to interpret when something in the personality has gone awry. But the dream as a literary artifice seems always to demand interpretation:

> Freed from pressures of strict chronology and verisimilitude, the unfolding of basic oppositions is unusually fluent and persuasive. This suggests that the traditional dream artifice in allegorical narratives disguises deliberate intention in the form of a mystery or seeming irrelevances; and this quality invariably invites interpretation.[7]

The artistic use of a dream, therefore, is likely to be a controlled departure from the limits of ordinary reality in order to trigger a special kind of interpretation, a more formal and rational perception of significance than the presentation of realistic details demands or allows for. Because dreams do not have the surface logic of realistic detail, they cannot be understood in themselves. Faced with an artistically created dream, the reader senses a challenge to discover the subterranean logic that holds the dream together. We suspect the presence of allegory when we find the normal canons of reality violated and we begin to look for a subterranean interpretation in order to see the logic of the whole.

We are now in a position to examine the third reason for Hawthorne's use of a historical setting. The story of "My Kinsman, Major Molineux" is set at a crucial moment in our national history. By the choice of this moment Hawthorne broadens the significance of Robin's story beyond the narrow bonds of psychological allegory and gives it the dimensions of a cultural memory. It is the dream of a society about its past—as ritual will appear as the dream of the Puritan society about its present in *The Scarlet Letter*. In other words, though it is true to say that history as history holds little interest for Hawthorne, it is not true to say that individual psychological and moral growth was the exclusive focus of his interest. Many of his stories are confined to a meaning within the psychology of the individual, but these stories tend to be out of time, or indifferent to it. "The Birthmark" or "Rappaccini's Daughter" are examples of this. But in the tales with a historical setting, Hawthorne is attempting to connect the past with the present, to show us the relevance of past national experience to present reality. That is why, having immersed us in the past, he likes to bring us explicitly back to the daylight world of the present. We have gained a new understanding of the present, of ourselves as individual persons within a concrete historical situation, from our literary dream of the past.

The basic structural technique which casts the aura of a dream over Robin's adventures is their presentation in a series of bizarre encounters which are systematic enough to show rational control. Colors are reduced to black and red. Successive circles of harsh, man-made light glare out of a pervasive background of dark, empty streets made unreal by the mysterious light of the moon.

The story opens within the clear circle of light from the ferryman's lantern. The scene is static, the writing purely descriptive. Robin then moves out of the lantern light into the dark town, only to be brought up short by the realization that he does not know where he is going. Robin catches sight of a man hurrying along and when both emerge into the full light of a barbershop, Robin asks for help. His question brings all activity to a halt. Then the stranger explodes with hostility and the barbershop explodes with laughter; Robin heads off puzzled again into the night. So it is with each adventure. A supper party at an inn makes another splash of light in the darkness. Robin enters the light, makes his simple request and is again mysteriously treated with hostility and laughter and left alone in a dark and narrow lane. He emerges once more into a brightly lit street where he is surrounded by promenading townspeople. But the "man of authority" whom he had first encountered at the barbershop once more frightens him back into darkness, the deserted, moonlit back streets of the city. The glare of scarlet illumines the scene with the prostitute. Robin seems to be drawing nearer to his goal until the watchman with his lantern frightens him off and sends a trailing cadence of drowsy laughter after him. Once more "the streets lay before him, strange and desolate, and the lights were extinguished in almost every house" (1215).

The individual scenes are realistic enough, but the whole series of encounters is made bizarre by the abrupt alternation of darkness and glaring light which divides the encounters into a series of discontinuous moments of stasis. This mode of development alerts the reader to the fact that the encounters are systematic, a rationally controlled survey of "all ranks and classes of the states."[8] Robin's journey shows him that for some mysterious reason he is the laughing stock of a whole hostile world. There is a final, climactic encounter, this one in the ambiguous moonlight:

But the man's complexion had undergone a singular, or, more properly, a two-fold change. One side of the face blazed an intense red, while the other was black as midnight, the division line being in the broad bridge of the nose; and a mouth which seemed to extend from ear to ear was black or red, in contrast to the color of the cheek. The effect was as if two individual devils, a fiend of fire and a fiend of darkness, had united themselves to form this infernal visage. (1216)

This is the peak of the series of visual shocks by which Hawthorne has presented Robin's search for his kinsman. It is a final and clear testimony to the fact that Robin's adventures are to be understood as a voyage to the underworld. Black and red are the colors of hell, and the man is both real and inhuman, man and devil, in a word, infernal.

At this point a new kind of structural unification begins to work. Robin gives up his search. There is a long, lonely moment during which Robin realizes that he has lost his grasp on reality. He cannot tell which is real, the homelife of the past from which he is shut out, or the hostile present which will not accept him. But Hawthorne keeps the story driving towards its climax, even during this long meditative interlude, by keeping us aware of the growing murmur of a crowd. This is the thread on which the rest of the tale is strung. The sound eventually becomes distinguishable as laughter. Then activity explodes all around Robin and the friend that he had just acquired. Windows are thrown open to greet the mounting uproar. The moonlight is colored by the more infernal red of a torchlight procession. All the colors of the night's adventures are assumed into this parade. Hawthorne interprets their meaning: "the red of one cheek was an emblem of fire and sword; the blackness of the other betokened the mourning that attends them" (1221). The whole march, says Hawthorne, has "a visionary air as if a dream had broken forth from some feverish brain, and were sweeping visibly through the midnight streets" (1221). Both sound and vision, shouts and trumpets, torches and moonlight clash together in a tremendous visual and audible cacophony, then burst over the black figure of Major Molineux. Again, everything stops. There is a moment of recognition between Robin and his kinsman. The night's adventures pass in review as each of its personalities appears as a party to the violence of the Major's fate. Then Robin ratifies the whole by his own laughter and the story is over.

For our purposes an allegorical interpretation of "My Kinsman, Major Molineux" is not necessary. There is a certain coherence to the combined efforts of critics who have. Rather the story illustrates some of Hawthorne's allegorical techniques. More of the allegorical techniques of this story will be treated in connection with the analysis of other stories. What we have seen here is the way Hawthorne uses a historical setting for the creation of a dream allegory, and how his use of a discontinuous serial structure of events suggests both the unreality of a dream and the strict linear development of a story which is under the control of conceptual thinking. In "Young Goodman Brown" there is a similar structure and a similar use of the past, as well as a fairly clear example of allegorical characterization.

Young Goodman Brown

"Young Goodman Brown" is like "My Kinsman, Major Molineux" in having a specific historical setting, but it does not have a historical introduction. Hawthorne begins immediately with his fictional realities, with the story. He does not first appeal to his reader's prejudice in favor of history, nor does he place himself clearly before the reader as a detached interpreter of the story. Within the narrative he alerts the reader to the fact that this is an allegory by playing upon the name Faith. We do not, then, begin with the contrast between actuality and fiction, as we did in "My Kinsman, Major Molineux." Still, the problem of the contrast between reality and dream is built into the structure of the story and affects its meaning as allegory.

There is nothing unreal about young Goodman Brown's departure from Faith and from his village, but as soon as he reaches the forest we are confronted with bolder violations of the canons of reality than we met in the nightmare experiences of Robin Molineux. The suggestion that Robin's journey was a dream journey was subtly made, by means of the stylized structure, the atmospheric effects of light and surrounding dark, and the unnerving repetition of meaningless laughter. Here, however, we learn that young Goodman Brown's companion has walked from Boston to Salem in fifteen minutes. We learn soon that he is an intimate friend of people long dead. Then, when he gives his staff to Goody Cloyse, she and the staff disappear. It is, however, only at the nightmare climax that we are forced to recognize that somewhere between the village and the forest there has been a shift from reality to dream. The scene of the Black Mass disappears with a totality possible only for a dream:

> "Faith! Faith!" cried the husband, "look up to heaven, and resist the wicked one."
> Whether Faith obeyed he knew not. Hardly had he spoken when he found himself amid calm night and solitude, listening to a roar of the wind which died heavily away through the forest. He staggered against the rock, and felt it chill and damp; while a hanging twig, that had been all on fire, besprinkled his cheek with the coldest dew. (1041)

But Hawthorne is not quite willing to leave it at that. He explicitly calls attention to the ambiguity of the experience: "Had Goodman Brown fallen asleep in the forest and only dreamed a wild dream of a witch-meeting?" (1042).

In other words, though this story is even less realistic than Robin Molineux's nightmare, there is a value for Hawthorne in sustaining a doubt about its reality. The important thing is not to decide whether young Goodman Brown has been through a real experience, but to realize that whatever the epistemological value of witches' meetings, what has happened to young Goodman

Brown can really happen to human beings and probably happened to many Puritans. "Young Goodman Brown" is not a dream narrative framed by the historical reflections of its author, as was "My Kinsman, Major Molineux," but it capitalizes on the same tension between reality and dream in order to emphasize the psychological reality of what was expressed in a dream.

There is another very important similarity between "Young Goodman Brown" and "My Kinsman, Major Molineux" in their use of a concrete historical setting. Both stories are psychological allegories. They narrate experiences that are typical of the experience of all men in any place or time. But, by placing them in actual periods of the American past, Hawthorne gives another dimension to their allegorical reference. By placing "My Kinsman, Major Molineux" in the revolutionary period, as we have seen, Hawthorne makes Robin's experience not only the universal psychological experience of every man who achieves adulthood, but also the image of a particular society achieving its psychological independence from the colonizing father. By placing "Young Goodman Brown" within the specific Puritan past of America, then, Hawthorne raises again a question that applies to the American experience. What has happened to us as a result of the Puritan experience? We are to read the story both as an allegory of the soul's confrontation with doubt and as an allegory about the Puritan faith.

The analogy between "Young Goodman Brown" and "My Kinsman, Major Molineux" holds true with respect to the structure of the two stories as well. There is the same stylized progress through darkness. The story line is built up from a series of encounters with the people who are most representative of a society and who indicate that the validity of the whole society is placed in question by young Goodman Brown's experience. When an author makes such a systematic survey of a society it is very difficult to believe that he is merely concerned with the reaction of one man to that society. In other words, a systematic survey of society indicates the allegorist's interest in society as the context for the intellectual or emotional reactions of the individual he places in opposition to it. As in "My Kinsman, Major Molineux," the wandering is climaxed by a final scene which gathers together all the characters encountered along the way, brings all the color

and sound motifs to a crescendo, and climaxes all by a startling
encounter between the two key characters. In "My Kinsman,
Major Molineux," it was an encounter between Robin and his
kinsman. Here it is Goodman Brown with, note, not Satan, but
Faith.

The use of a name like Faith in contexts which play upon both
the person and the theological concept is the most basic kind of
allegorical technique. "Young Goodman Brown" is clearly a
"twice-told tale," Edwin Honig's phrase borrowed from Hawthorne, for allegory. An old story must be so thoroughly recon-
ceived and recreated by the new telling of it as to give the new
story an authority of its own, independent of the authority of
the old story.[9] The old story here is, of course, the story of the
fall of Adam through the temptation of Eve. But Eve is renamed
Faith, which gives a daring new irony to this new story of the
fall of man. On the level of the historically plausible, Faith is,
for Goodman Brown, the center and source of domestic tran-
quility, Hawthorne's touchstone for all that has the ring of health
and reality. But as we move into the dream narrative, she begins
to take on the conceptual religious value of her name: "Faith
kept me back a while" (1034), says Goodman Brown to the
devil. Young Goodman Brown's adventure into the wilderness
is a gradual awakening to the fact that his father and his father's
fathers had consorted with the devil, that officials of the Church
and other pillars of Christian virtue were the devil's close friends.
Consequently, the whole of religious life, based on faith, is called
into question. The devil at first disclaims all power over Faith:
"I would not for twenty old women like the one hobbling before
us that Faith should come to any harm" (1035). Goodman
Brown continues to invoke her saving influence: "What if a
wretched old woman do choose to go to the devil when I thought
she was going to heaven: is that any reason why I should quit
my dear Faith and go after her?" (1036-37). "With heaven
above and Faith below, I will yet stand firm against the devil!"
The play on the protestant theological doctrine of Faith as a virtue which includes trust and confidence and which is the all-
embracing rule of religious life is clearly and smoothly implied
in words which, even so, can be understood as merely the expression of marital fidelity. Because the theological meaning of

the name Faith has been so firmly implied, Goodman Brown's agony at the sound of his wife's voice in the company of those going to the witches' meeting is, besides being a shattering event on the level of surface narrative, an agony about the very possibility of sincere belief. It is not just the hypocrisy of a whole community of pseudo-Christians that haunts Goodman Brown, but the possibility that his Faith, the foundation of all religion as he knows it, is merely a form of hypocrisy and devil worship: " 'My Faith is gone!' cried he, after one stupefied moment. 'There is no good on earth; and sin is but a name. Come, devil; for to thee is this world given' " (1038). There is one more moment of desperate hope when Goodman Brown does not see Faith at the meeting. But almost immediately she appears beside him at the devil's altar: "the wretched man beheld his Faith" (1041).

As we have already seen, Hawthorne preserves an ambiguity about the presence of Faith at the meeting in order to emphasize the reality of the scar left on young Goodman Brown by this night's terrible confrontation, not with the devil but with her.

> Often, awaking suddenly at midnight, he shrank from the bosom of Faith; . . . . And when he had lived long, and was borne to his grave a hoary corpse, followed by Faith, an aged woman, and children and grandchildren, a goodly procession, besides neighbors not a few, they carved no hopeful verse upon his tombstone, for his dying hour was gloom. (1042)

We see, in the play of ambiguity around the name and character of Faith, that Hawthorne, in order to create a special kind of interpretative alertness in his reader, has sacrificed the interest in Faith as a growing human character, to create an allegorical character. The artistry is in the fact that Hawthorne never allows us to turn loose of the reality of the human figure, but keeps her tantalizingly before us as he plays with the theological concept of Faith.[10]

What is it that Hawthorne has sacrificed, in sacrificing a mimetic realism in the creation of the character of Faith?

As we usually understand human agency, we think that the psychologically or behaviorally natural sort of character type

is that of a person who appears capable of making decisions
(who "knows what he wants," can deliberate about means toward this end) and also, and this is equally important, who is
capable of "growing."[11]

The author of an allegory, then, tries to tip the balance of our
interest away from what the character is becoming and toward
what the character means. Since the allegorical character is the
representation of a concept—an entity which can develop, but
cannot reverse itself—so it is normal that his actions proceed
not from choices, but from a certain stable commitment which
is determined by what he means in allegory. Faith makes no
choices in "Young Goodman Brown." The story reaches its climax when Goodman Brown begs her to make a choice, but at
that point the nightmare disappears. Young Goodman Brown
is horrified at the possibility that his Faith might mean commitment to the devil, and his extreme fear makes him wake up before
he can find out. He is never sure whether his Faith is equal to the
encounter with the devil, as, for Hawthorne, Calvinism was
never sure. We will see this same ambiguity at the heart of Calvinism embodied in Dimmesdale in The Scarlet Letter.

Does young Goodman Brown make a choice? Brown is the
representative Puritan who must go through the basic human
encounter with evil. Whether to do so or not is not really left to
him to decide. It is the unavoidable crisis in human maturation.
We are given here, in other words, not the tragedy of a man
who has chosen to look at evil, but the destruction of a man whose
Puritan faith is unequal to the inevitable encounter with evil.

That young Goodman Brown is not free is only subtly suggested at first. Hawthorne insists, as a true allegorist should, on
the realistic surface of his allegory. Still, as young Goodman
Brown cajoles his wife's consent, the question is not whether or
not he will go to the forest, but an anxious fear lest Faith may
find out what he is about. That is, Goodman Brown must face
evil, there is no question about that. But to do so, he must put
his Faith behind him because of his fear that Faith is not equal
to man's necessary encounter with evil. Hawthorne plays long
and deliberately with Goodman Brown's sense that he can yet
escape the devil, even climaxing it with the exclamation, "With

heaven above and Faith below, I will yet stand firm against the devil!" (1038). The point is that Faith is not below. He has abandoned her in order to face evil. The devil is, of course, quite confident that young Goodman Brown must eventually follow him. But it is because of the kind of faith he has, that young Goodman Brown cannot see evil calmly. It is a faith that he feels must be abandoned if he is to confront the experience of evil.

Still, we do not feel young Goodman Brown as an automaton moving inexorably through a world of dream. To hold our interest, he must seem to be a man at grips with the ambiguities of human choice. But choice is not the point of allegory, as it is of tragedy. Once one looks at the moments of choice here, one sees that they are not real options. The issue is one of meaning, young Goodman Brown as the representative of Puritanism. In him we see the helplessness of Puritan faith to deal successfully with the universality of evil. What Hawthorne is saying is that to those who insist, as do the Puritans that the world be seen as black and white, blackness is the vision that will prevail. The fault is with the Puritan view of life, not with the strength of the hero.

On the literal level of the story we may be tempted to say that there was a moment at which Goodman Brown went astray, the moment, for example, in which he turned from Faith to enter the forest. But to recognize the fact that once he is in the forest evil becomes more and more clearly the prevailing moral color of the world, is to see that there was something in the very nature of his Faith that made it unreconcilable with the existence of evil. Goodman Brown's dream experience is his initiation into a reality that no choice could have helped him avoid, and that his Faith made him incapable of accepting.

> Typifying the [dream-allegory] procedure is a guiding, usually beneficent intelligence that impels and even shares the hero's consciousness. Sometimes it is that part of divinity present in each man, or it is the corrective effects which reason and imagination can have upon the consciousness. . . .
> Since the Renaissance such an intelligence seeks to bring authority closer to actual social and psychological needs than medieval doctrine allowed.[12]

There is a guide in each of the two stories we have been considering. They are the friendly stranger who waits with Robin for his kinsman, and Satan in the shape of Goodman Brown's father. Robin's guide is benevolent, exercising an almost therapeutic function. He plays down the magnitude of things: "there do appear to be three or four riotous fellows abroad tonight" (1220). He keeps Robin to his purpose when he is tempted to follow the crowd for the fun of it: "Sit down again, sit down, good Robin, ... You forget that we must wait here for your kinsman; ...." (1220). He conducts Robin through the crucial transition from his dream experience into the world of reality: " 'Well, Robin, are you dreaming?' " (1222). And he stands at Robin's side to support him in making his decision about the future:

> "Some few days hence, if you wish it, I will send you on your journey. Or, if you prefer to remain with us, perhaps, as you are a shrewd youth, you may rise in the world without the help of your kinsman, Major Molineux." (1223)

The friendly stranger, then, is a kind of incarnation of Robin's healthy self, the adult who will emerge from this experience purified and ready for life. He is the opposite of what Robin's kinsman would have been. He is detached but interested, helpful for the matter at hand, but careful not to interfere with Robin's choice.

The experience of Robin is a liberating experience. Young Goodman Brown, on the other hand, is delivered into a kind of slavery, a slavery not to Satan, but to the evil-obsessed hypocrisy of the religion of his fathers. Another difference is that for young Goodman Brown there are two guides. Faith is the guide he abandons; Satan is the guide that assumes control.[13] Hawthorne stresses their similarities enough to suggest that Satan is Brown's double. He assumes the appearance of Goodman Brown's father. And their identity extends even to their thinking: Satan discoursed so "aptly that his arguments seemed rather to spring up in the bosom of his auditor than to be suggested by himself" (1036).

"Young Goodman Brown," then, is, like "My Kinsman, Major Molineux," an allegory which uses the material of history in order to give the dimension of cultural significance along with the dimension of psychological and moral meaning. Both stories have the same basic serial structure of discontinuous encounters with the representatives of a society. But in "Young Goodman Brown" we encounter more clearly allegorical characters, personages whose meaning is more important than their growth, and who are mirrored by the characters who surround them.

The Maypole of Merry Mount

The interaction of reality and dream, which we have seen in "My Kinsman, Major Molineux" and "Young Goodman Brown" appears in yet another form in "The Maypole of Merry Mount." Hawthorne uses again the technique of the historical essay. But also and more important, he brings the conflict between reality and dream explicitly into the thematic center of this story.

Let us look first at the way Hawthorne uses the historical essay. In "The Maypole of Merry Mount" the historical essay appears in the center of the story. It acts as a fulcrum on which are balanced the two divisions of the dream narrative: the description of Midsummer Eve and the Puritan assault. Because he begins, as in "Young Goodman Brown," with his fictional realities, Hawthorne's eventual use of the historical essay seems necessarily more formal than in "My Kinsman, Major Molineux," where he began with his essay. Its impact here is more abrupt and draws more attention to itself:

> Now leave we the priest to marry them, and the masquers to sport round the Maypole, till the last sunbeam be withdrawn from its summit, and the shadows of the forest mingle gloomily in the dance. Meanwhile, we may discover who these gay people were. (885)

Such a clear separation of story and history signals the allegorist at work giving his interpretation of fictional events. As a technique this kind of stop-action is, we shall see, characteristic of the allegorical narrative style of *The Scarlet Letter*. But it is more than a technique. It is thematic, part of the meaning of the story, perhaps more clearly so than in the other two stories we have considered. There are critics, we have seen, who minimize Hawthorne's interest in history and insist that his allegories are exclusively psychological, allegories of the heart, for instance, Frederick Crews:

> When we look for the thematic common denominator between the overtly historical fiction and such equally Hawthornian, but ahistorical, tales as "Wakefield," "Ethan Brand," and "The Birthmark," we find that Hawthorne's interest in history is only a special case of his interest in fathers and sons, guilt and retribution, instinct and inhibition. . . . The history of the nation interests him *only* as it is metaphorical of individual mental strife.[14]

This is a typical weakness of the psychoanalytic approach. Society is important only as a screen onto which one projects individual conflict. But if all that interests Hawthorne is individual mental strife, there would be no need for him to try to give any special reality or historical authenticity to the people of Merry Mount. This, however, is precisely the purpose of his interpolated historical essay. The people of Merry Mount have a recognizable human psychology of pleasure; they come from real classes of people who were seen in London streets: minstrels, wandering players, "mirth-makers of every sort." Their customs are the customs of Old England; and their emblem, the maypole, has its roots in actual popular tradition. Hawthorne is interested both in individual psychology and in the cultural psychology of the nation. It is certainly true, as Crews says, that the common denominator between the historical and the ahistorical fiction is Hawthorne's interest in individual mental strife. But that which is specific to the historical tales is Hawthorne's interest in the further dimension of national experience. By means of a historical essay, then, Hawthorne creates an important tension between real people and allegorical characters. He establishes the fact that Merry Mount was a real place at a real time in history; and that makes his actuality-minded readers more willing to accept his story, and more serious in their attempt to get at its meaning.

Let us go on, then, to consider the fact that in this story the central thematic concern is the conflict between reality and dream. The characteristic fact about Merry Mount is that to Hawthorne it is a historical reality rooted in time, while to its citizens it is a world set apart from time and change:

> But May, or her mirthful spirit, dwelt all the year round at Merry Mount, sporting with the Summer months, and revelling with Autumn, and basking in the glow of Winter's fireside. (882)

When the May Lord reproaches the Lady of the May for her pensive looks, she answers in terms of dream and reality: "I struggle as with a dream, and fancy that these shapes of our jovial friends are visionary and their mirth unreal, and that we are no true Lord and Lady of the May" (884). Merry Mount, then, is an attempt to make real the unreal world of a dream. Consequently it is, Hawthorne himself interjects, an empty world for those such as the Lord and Lady of the May, who indulge in as real a thing as love:

> No sooner had their hearts glowed with real passion, than they were sensible of something vague and unsubstantial in their former pleasures, and felt a dreary presentiment of inevitable change. From the moment that they truly loved, they had subjected themselves to earth's doom of care and sorrow, and troubled joy, and had no more a home at Merry Mount. (885)

The Puritans consider themselves the realists. When they appear at Merry Mount they are like "waking thoughts" which "start up amid the scattered fantasies of a dream" (887). Endicott is wrought of iron—an interesting American image for the "really real"; and "no fantastic foolery could look him in the face" (887).

Hawthorne stands clearly on both sides of this opposition; he makes it clear that one must reject the unreality of Merry Mount; but he balances this with a less elaborate though equally clear rejection of the Puritans. They are "dismal wretches":

> Their weapons were always at hand, to shoot down the straggling savage. When they met in conclave, it was never to keep

up the old English mirth, but to hear sermons three hours
long, or to proclaim bounties on the heads of wolves and the
scalps of Indians. (886)

Hawthorne rejects both the votaries of the dream and the
guardians of reality by looking at each from the point of view
of the other. There is even a certain question about the "realism"
of the Puritans. They are themselves "victims of a total delusory
system, peopling the woods with devils," as Crews has pointed
out.[15] One may wonder why an allegory so clearly concerned with
rival systems of value fails to opt for either one. Here the nature
of allegory as a "twice-told tale" comes to our aid.

The tale that Hawthorne is re-telling here is, once more, the
story of the fall. Hawthorne at one point suggests that Merry
Mount was a kind of Eden: "O, people of the Golden Age, the
chief of your husbandry was to raise flowers!" (883). Such irre-
sponsibility turns out to be grotesque, and joy is only the mask of
a deeper despair:

> The young deemed themselves happy. The elder spirits, if they
> knew that mirth was but the counterfeit of happiness, yet fol-
> lowed the false shadow wilfully, because at least her garments
> glittered brightest. Sworn triflers of a lifetime, they would not
> venture among the sober truths of life not even to be truly
> blest. (885)

Unfortunately the only alternative, the reality into which fallen
man descends when his Eden is destroyed, is the dismal world of
Puritanism, cruel, violent, unjust, unrelieved by any expression of
the joy of human life and the tenderness of love. What Hawthorne
has done in retelling the scriptural story is to shift the issue completely. The Fall, in Genesis, is an explanation in narrative form
for human perversity and human suffering. That story affirmed
that man belonged in a better state and had lost it by his own
fault. This story is a new story with its own thematic center. It
talks, not about the loss of an abstract ideal state, but about the
necessary loss of a concrete and, for a time at least, real state;
that is, the childhood world. The question Hawthorne is answer-
ing, then, is not: why do men suffer; it is, rather, why must man
face up to the fact of suffering. It is the allegory of maturity

once more, not the allegory of right and wrong, and it applies both to the individual and to the nation.

The salient feature of the narrative technique of "The Maypole of Merry Mount" is its lack of action. Only one thing happens, the invasion of Merry Mount, and that is merely a matter of moments; the Puritans step from the forest and the world of dream and mirth collapses. Most of the sketch is spent in setting up and elaborating the visual contrast between the two worlds of Merry Mount and the Puritans. This tendency to develop a static opposition in visual, contemplative terms, is a second logical strategy of allegory. The first allegories we saw had a serial structure. They were built of successive encounters with the representatives of society. Here there is no movement, and little action. The structure is dialectical. The two societies are summarized in symbols and are juxtaposed almost geometrically in concentric circles. At the center of the world of Merry Mount is the elaborately ornamented maypole. Around it is its circle of demi-humans. In the outer darkness which surrounds the circle of maypole votaries is the forest peopled with shadowy and hostile Puritans. Because this false Eden and its fall is the principle focus of Hawthorne's interest, it receives the greatest elaboration. But the other world of Puritanism is given a like circular structure. The whipping post "might be termed the Puritan Maypole" (886), and surrounding it is the grim troop of Puritans. Moreover, outside this circle of Puritans there is a corresponding outer darkness:

> The Puritans affirmed, that, when a psalm was pealing from their place of worship, the echo which the forest sent them back, seemed often like the chorus of a jolly catch, closing with a roar of laughter. (886)

Hawthorne's task as narrator, then, is not the unfolding of an action but the elaboration of this visual, dialectical opposition between rival moral forces: "Jollity and gloom were contending for an empire" (882).

When action is reduced to a virtual standstill, descriptive characterization and imagery remain as modes of development. Hawthorne has here chosen imagery, not metaphor, but decoration. Metaphor is meant to give, by its immediacy, a more vivid portrayal of reality. Decoration picks objects out, sets them off from their surroundings in a kind of splendid isolation, and pushes the reader toward interest in their meaning instead of their reality. The maypole is singled out this way both by Hawthorne's lavish detail and by the fact that no other feature of the place is even mentioned. Nothing is allowed to distract from this central symbol in the center of the forest clearing. It is given a kind of personality—as though it were an idol. It had preserved "the slender grace of youth" while equalling the "loftiest heights of the old wood monarchs." Flowers "laugh" from its branches; it is a "happy pine tree." The maypole is further isolated from the natural landscape in which it grew by the bizarre rout of "monsters" who exist around it in a kind of static choreography. The only action at Merry Mount is the dance, and the only place is around the maypole.

The decorated monsters are set off from the world of ordinary humanity by the way in which Hawthorne talks of them: as though they really were half beast, half human rather than merely costumed that way. They are story-book people, "fauns and nymphs" or "gothic monsters" driven from their homes in ancient fable. They stand out against the dark forest background, visually isolated by their incongruity: "There was the likeness of a bear erect, brute in all but his hind legs, which were adorned with pink silk stockings." The emphasis on the grotesque continues:

> Other faces wore the similitude of man or woman, but distorted or extravagant, with red noses pendulous before their mouths, which seemed of awful depth, and stretched from ear to ear in an eternal fit of laughter. (883)

The effect is the same as is given by the exaggerated contrast of light and shadow in the surrealist scenery of "My Kinsman, Major Molineux." The function served by heightening detail with distortion is again to excite the reader's faculty of interpretation. The desire for realism is consistently frustrated. The reader is drawn instead to contemplate static and vividly ornamented objects arranged in a system. Once awakened to the fact that mimetic naturalism is not the purpose of the narrative, the reader must find in concept the significance that will explain how such wild fantasy can be part of a unified artistic presentation. He must, in other words, seek out the conceptual values which the flamboyant decor and visual arrangement of objects in a system is meant to signify.

Because of this concern with values, the esthetic justification for Hawthorne's emphasis on bizarre decoration is partly a rhetorical justification. An allegorist makes a value judgment by means of his ornamentation; and that is a rhetorical enterprise. Consequently the highly contrasted decoration by which the static opposition of circles is developed serves much more than to excite the reader's enjoyment of colorful detail. The bright colors and reckless abandon of Merry Mount are pleasant enough to imagine. But while we enjoy, Hawthorne is stating his values, making his point. The people of Merry Mount, half-way decked out as animals, are expressing their own violation of the order of nature. After describing in literal terms the half-human, half-animal colonists, he suddenly reverses the point of view to drive his point more securely home. He introduces a real bear, whose "inferior nature rose half way to meet his companions as they stooped" (883). There is clearly an ordered scale of being, for Hawthorne, which the colonists of Merry Mount have broken. This is hardly a picture of the harmony between man and nature, as Q. D. Leavis interprets.[16] Hawthorne leaves no doubts about his values:

Had a wanderer, bewildered in the melancholy forest, heard their mirth, and stolen a half-affrighted glance, he might have fancied them the crew of Comus, some already transformed to brutes, some midway between man and beast, and the others rioting in the flow of tipsy jollity that foreran the change. (883)

Hawthorne is saying that the force that creates Merry Mount is the regressive drive toward the inhuman and the irresponsible.

But, says Hawthorne in the next sentence, the Puritans are just as incapable of grasping the nature of the disorder of Merry Mount as are its colonists. Though they may be closer to reality, Hawthorne never endows them with any surplus of insight: "But a band of Puritans, who watched the scene, invisible themselves, compared the masques to those devils and ruined souls with whom their superstition peopled the black wilderness" (883).

The Puritans are not so elaborately decked with value-laden ornamentation but they are decisively situated on the same scale of values. They toil through the woods with animal-like stoicism "each with a horseload of iron armor to burden his footsteps" (886). And the cruelty, violence, and meanness which Hawthorne goes on to describe takes on an aura of beastliness. The Puritans are surrounded by or trapped in their own armor. They are "men of iron," a cut below the animal in their lack of human qualities. Hawthorne's use of ornamental imagery, lavish in the case of the colonists of Merry Mount, and sparing in the case of the Puritans, serves his rhetorical purpose of showing the basic disorder inherent in both systems.

In spite of the fact that "The Maypole of Merry Mount" is almost totally static, there is some action; and there are, consequently, protagonists. They are not, however, allowed to disturb the schematic simplicity of the opposition between the Puritans and Merry Mount. At the center is the pair of young lovers. They are, at first, colonists of Merry Mount, costumed appropriately, though with greater dignity, as the central figures of the colony's ritual. On either side of this couple, contending for the right to shape their marriage according to one or other of the conflicting ways of life, are two guides: the priest and the Puritan of Puritans.

The priest is grotesquely ornamented in a special way. He seemed "the wildest monster" there, but his monstrosity is not the degrading mixture of animal and human. Rather, he upsets a much higher order than the order of nature. He is both "canonically dressed" and "decked with flowers in heathen fashion." He is a deliberate reversion to paganism. It is the "riot of his rolling eye, and the pagan decorations of his holy garb" which make him the "Comus of the crew"—the leader in upsetting the right order of things. His gospel is "a dance, to show the youthful pair what life is made of, and how airily they should go through it" (884).

The Puritan leader is equally conspicuous and typical of the way of life he represents, though here also less is done with decorative imagery as a means of underlining his function in the story. The iron-like quality of his personality exhausts his character:

> So stern was the energy of his aspect, that the whole man, visage, frame, and soul, seemed wrought of iron, gifted with life and thought, yet all of one substance with his headpiece and breastplate. (887)

Here, more than in either of the two stories discussed before, we have the picture of the typical allegorical agent, whose human qualities are so reduced that they seemed to be consumed by the function or force, the meaning he represents. The multivalent tendencies of human nature have been sacrificed, in the creation of these characters, to the stability of natures rooted in basic commitments to rival values, in this case, the values of the dream and the values of reality. Neither Endicott nor the priest makes choices. They follow, rather, the determinism of their respective commitments. The glimmer of sympathy that Endicott shows for the Lord and Lady of the May seems to be the glimmer of interest that would be aroused in such a man by the possibility of turning them into versions of himself. Caught between two such agents, the Lord and Lady of the May merely submit to the power of the stronger.

We do not find this simplification of human dimension unsatisfying, however. For one thing, instead of being faced with a complex character, we are faced with incarnations of warring tendencies. In other words, complexity is there, but incarnate in several characters rather than merely in one. Secondly, we have been given enough clues to the guiding allegorical form of the story to recognize that the development of character is not Hawthorne's basic concern, but the development of meaning. The accumulated effect of a whole battery of allegorical techniques has alerted us and brought our powers of intellectual interpretation into play. It will be clearer, perhaps, as more of these allegorical techniques come to light, that the more or less conscious realization that there is a consistent allegorical intention behind Hawthorne's violations of realism is the reason that criticisms of his characterization seem to miss the mark. Whether we realize it or not, he has persuaded us to accept his genre of writing. We catch on to his allegorical vision and everything seems right.

The Gray Champion

In "The Gray Champion," the feint in the direction of history is hardly a feint. There is no transition to an allegorical dream world; there is only, at the end, an aura of legend surrounding the Gray Champion himself.

But where was the Gray Champion? Some reported that, when the troops had gone from King Street, and the people were thronging tumultuously in their rear, Bradstreet, the aged Governor, was seen to embrace a form more aged than his own. Others soberly affirmed, that while they marvelled at the venerable grandeur of his aspect, the old man had faded from their eyes, melting slowly into the hues of twilight, till, where he stood, there was an empty space. But all agreed that the hoary shape was gone. The men of that generation watched for his reappearance, in sunshine and in twilight, but never saw him more, nor knew when his funeral passed, nor where his gravestone was. (866)

Hawthorne has been able, in this story, to create an allegory without abandoning the narrative stance of the historical essayist. He interjects the legendary figure of the Gray Champion into an entirely plausible confrontation between the people and their colonial rulers and, at the end, gives him an allegorical meaning:

He is the type of New England's hereditary spirit; and his shadowy march, on the eve of danger, must ever be the pledge, that New England's sons will vindicate their ancestry. (866)

Hawthorne uses the word *type* here apparently with no consciousness of any distinction between allegory based on abstraction and biblical allegory based on historical events and people and called *typology* by biblical scholars. Biblical typology is based upon the faith of the biblical author that God is guiding history and that God makes his divine purpose clear to men in the pattern of events. The faith of the author allows him to perceive in historical events such a pattern as reveals to him the meaning and direction of history. Hawthorne has no very clear faith in the divine guidance of history, and so it is not surprising that his Gray Champion is not a historical figure but the personification of an abstract quality of the Puritan spirit. Still, Hawthorne perceives this abstract quality in and through events of history:

> I have heard, that whenever the descendants of the Puritans are to show the spirit of their sires, the old man appears again. When eighty years had passed, he walked once more in King Street [the Boston Massacre]. Five years later, in the twilight of an April morning, he stood on the green, beside the meeting-house, at Lexington, where now the obelisk of granite, with a slab of slate inlaid, commemorates the first fallen of the Revolution. And when our fathers were toiling at the breastwork on Bunker's hill, all through that night the old warrior walked his rounds. (886)

Hawthorne's perception, then, though it is not the faith-inspired perception of the biblical writer, is infused with a conviction that the events of the Puritan past are an authentic and still vital historical force. He comes very close to a typological view of history here, which argues quite clearly, it seems to me, the fact that he was committed in some way to a kind of faith in the enduring quality of that history.

We are faced again with evidence for the fact that the culture of the Puritan past was no handy refuge for an allegorist who could not face the cold realities of his contemporary world—no matter what Hawthorne may say about himself in "The Custom-House." Hawthorne did not go to the past because it was distant and he could subject it to an arbitrary manipulation and so teach moral and psychological lessons he had learned outside the context of the past. For Hawthorne the past was near because it was still alive. As the past spoke to the biblical writer about his own present, the American past of Hawthorne taught him the am-

biguous lessons he teaches us in the allegories he writes about it.
As Professor Charles Feidelson has said, the Puritans are the
starting point of Hawthorne's thought. He is not just using them
as people about whom he can write stories; he is wrestling with
their problems.[17]

Hawthorne seems, then, to have assumed the role of public
poet or spokesman for his culture, more specifically, for its Puritan heritage. However, he is a much less committed spokesman
than, say, Dante or Spenser were for their cultures. For example,
in "The Gray Champion" Hawthorne pushes himself forward
editorially with an unusual eagerness. He is understandably concerned about "our liberties," but his concern for "our religion"
seems somewhat forced in the light of his usual ambivalence
toward Puritanism. Hawthorne continues to use "our" rather
insistently throughout the introductory passage, which leads one
to the conclusion that he felt a certain guilt about his ambivalence.
He seems to be trying desperately to establish a bond with his
readers, to assume, perhaps, the position of public poet by expressing more of a sense of public responsibility. But ambiguity
always prevails.

Here is Hawthorne's description of the crowd of colonists in
"The Gray Champion":

> There were the sober garb, the general severity of mien, the
> gloomy but undismayed expression, the scriptural forms of
> speech, and the confidence in Heaven's blessing on a righteous
> cause, which would have marked a band of the original Puri-
> tans, when threatened by some peril of the wilderness. (862)

The qualities listed here are value-laden, but the values are
ambiguous. We see that ambiguity burst clearly into the open as
Hawthorne begins to sketch in the historical dimensions of the
crowd:

> There were men in the street that day who had worshipped
> there beneath the trees, before a house was reared to the God
> for whom they had become exiles. Old soldiers of the Parlia-
> ment were here, too, smiling grimly at the thought that their
> aged arms might strike another blow against the house of
> Stuart. Here, also, were the veterans of King Philip's war, who

had burned villages and slaughtered young and old, with pious fierceness, while the godly souls throughout the land were helping them with prayer. (862)

As in "The Maypole of Merry Mount," Hawthorne clearly rejects the royalist side of the dialectic, but only grudgingly accepts the other. When we come to the conclusion of the story, with its allegorical interpretation of the Gray Champion, we find the same ambiguity about the Puritan hero.

Long, long may it be, ere he comes again! His hour is one of darkness, and adversity, and peril. But should domestic tyranny oppress us, or the invader's step pollute our soil, still may the Gray Champion come, for he is the type of New England's hereditary spirit; and his shadowy march, on the eve of danger, must ever be the pledge, that New England's sons will vindicate their ancestry. (866)

According to Frederick Crews,

The Gray Champion . . . is anything but an epitome of democracy. . . . He is the image of a patriarch, and it is this image alone that wins the day. The whole tale could be described as a contest of paternal figures . . . all vying to exploit the colonists' "Filial love which had invariably secured their allegiance to the mother country."[18]

Hawthorne, then, belabors the ambiguity of Puritanism from every angle: The story of young Goodman Brown shows us the inability of Puritanism to confront the fact of evil without abandoning faith. It is this which is behind the hard realism and sobriety of the Puritan people. In "The Maypole of Merry Mount" we see the Puritan spirit measured against those who opt for an opposite joy. We are forced in spite of ourselves to bow to the superior realism of that very guilt-ridden and inhuman sect. In "The Gray Champion" Puritanism's political superiority is grudgingly granted precisely because it respects, or at least demands, the high human right of freedom. But we have seen, in this story as well as in "My Kinsman, Major Molineux," how a harsh and cruel violence infects the very valid human striving for freedom. It is this ambivalence towards the Puritanism of which he makes himself the spokesman which gives to Hawthorne's stories of his native land, it seems to me, the peculiar intensity which surrounds them. He did not need the antique romantic associations of Europe, even though he complained of not having them. He was able, instead, to write valid and compelling allegory about a Puritanism that still lived on. Hawthorne, it seems, carried on a kind of public examination of conscience, one which Puritanism itself had failed to engage in. Hawthorne, though accepting the role of spokesman for the culture descended from Puritanism, is forced himself, and forces his fellow Americans to see both the values and the evils of the past from which they have all come. Allegory works, then, in Hawthorne because, though it is story-telling with a thematic purpose, the purpose is to investigate, to test, not to propagandize. It is what Angus Fletcher calls a research project with, in this case, the Puritan heritage of American life as its boundaries. It involved, for Hawthorne, the constant risk of discovering that the whole thing was and remained evil. Hawthorne is more involved than his cool prose would make one think.

The allegory of "The Gray Champion" is constructed, like that of "The Maypole of Merry Mount," out of a dialectical opposition between rival forces. In this story, however, the dialectic moves. The first two paragraphs of "The Gray Champion" present the problem symmetrically; the first paragraph tells of the oppressive wrongs to the colony perpetrated by the administration of Sir Edmund Andros. The second paragraph describes the counter force at work, the resistance that begins to stir among the people at the news of the enterprise of the Prince of Orange. After this introductory stand-off, the next several paragraphs are devoted to the gathering of the Puritan crowd. Hawthorne uses the roll of the drum to set his narrative in motion. It will be the thread of continuity building suspense through the alternating descriptions, as was the murmur of the crowd in the latter half of "My Kinsman, Major Molineux."

Though he does not use imagery to set up a hierarchical arrangement among the Puritans, Hawthorne is careful to arrange them hierarchically. He forms them into small groups protectively surrounding their ministers, and brings them all to a unity around the figure of Governor Bradstreet, who appears "on the elevated steps of a door" to exhort them to order. The crowd is as ordered and orderly as the procession of soldiers which is marching to meet it. That is the balance which Hawthorne's allegorical imagination sets out to achieve: one ordered, symbolic army facing another.

Hawthorne uses a louder and deeper roll of the drum to increase suspense while bringing us back to the other side of the dialectic:

> All this time, the roll of the drum had been approaching through Cornhill, louder and deeper, till with reverberations from house to house, and the regular tramp of martial footsteps, it burst into the street. A double rank of soldiers made their appearance, occupying the whole breadth of the passage, with shouldered matchlocks, and matches burning, so as to present a row of fires in the dusk. Their steady march was like the progress of a machine, that would roll irresistibly over everything in its way. (863)

The image of the machine is obvious enough. It implies that the royal forces are amoral, but it heightens the suspense by making them irresistible as well. The allegorical style resides in the very explicitness of these techniques. Allegorical rhetoric does not want to be so suggestive as not to be clear.

Hawthorne brings the royalist leaders into the scene in such a way as to suggest that the machinelike order of the approaching army is a facade for a basic disorder:

> Next, moving slowly, with a confused clatter of hoofs on the pavement, rode a party of mounted gentlemen, the central figure being Sir Edmund Andros, elderly, but erect and soldier-like. Those around him were his favorite councillors, and the bitterest foes of New England. At his right hand rode Edward Randolph, our arch-enemy, that "blasted wretch," as Cotton Mather calls him, who achieved the downfall of our ancient government, and was followed with a sensible curse, through life and to his grave. On the other side was Bullivant, scattering jests and mockery as he rode along. Dudley came behind, with a downcast look, dreading, as well he might, to meet the indignant gaze of the people, who beheld him, their only countryman by birth, among the oppressors of his native land. (863)

Finally, in symmetrical opposition to the godly ministers of the Puritan crowd, comes the representative of royal religion, whose clothing is the symbolic focal point of Puritan hatred, as it was in "The Maypole of Merry Mount."

> But the figure which most attracted the public eye, and stirred up the deepest feeling, was the Episcopal clergyman of King's Chapel, riding haughtily among the magistrates in his priestly vestments, the fitting representatives of prelacy and persecution, the union of church and state, and all those abominations which had driven the Puritans to the wilderness. (863)

Finally, Hawthorne brings his dialectical movement to a complete stop while he sums up the whole picture in explicit allegorical interpretation:

> The whole scene was a picture of the condition of New England, and its moral, the deformity of any government that does not grow out of the nature of things and the character of the people. On one side the religious multitude, with their sad visages and dark attire, and on the other, the group of despotic rulers, with the high churchman in the midst, and here and there a crucifix at their bosoms, all magnificently clad, flushed with wine, proud of unjust authority, and scoffing at the universal groan. And the mercenary soldiers, waiting but the word to deluge the street with blood, showed the only means by which obedience could be secured. (863)

At this point Hawthorne is ready to intrude the figure of the Gray Champion. He does so with a biblical cry: "O Lord of Hosts, provide a Champion for thy people!" The symmetry of opposing forces leaves an open space into which the Gray Champion emerges. Again the development of the action is dialectical. As the Gray Champion advances, the Puritan crowd is struck with wonder; and when he orders the royal forces to stand, a "shout of awe and exultation" rises from the crowd. Then it is the turn of the royal party to question and challenge him. This is the "battle," the purely verbal *agon* of Greek drama. The Gray Champion delivers the final blow when he proclaims the fall of James. The royal governor must beat his retreat. The battle is fought and won in pure symbol. After two such battles some reflections on allegorical action in general will be appropriate.

Mimetic action, as opposed to allegorical action, is bound to the probable and usually foreswears sudden or irrational change. The prime concern in mimetic action is growth and, at crucial moments, decision. In allegorical action, on the other hand, the agents involved are less bound to the law of nature. They are representative figures and follow the laws of the concept or class which they represent. In the stories we have seen so far, the characters, instead of manifesting the moral and psychological growth of real human persons, have suffered the changes imposed upon them. Though there is a gradual build up to the transformations which take place, one has the impression of a sudden change at the climax of the action with little accompanying freedom to resist on the part of the hero. Robin of "My Kinsman, Major Molineux" is suddenly confronted with the shocking vision of his kinsman in the power of an angry mob, and he bursts into involuntary laughter. This is not the realistic culmination of a long-developing breakdown in his relationship with his kinsman, but the emergence of an every-man from the dream of youth, under the battering force of reality. Young Goodman Brown goes off into the forest suffering progressive attacks upon his faith. The final attack, when he suddenly sees Faith at his side at the devil's ritual, finishes the transformation which makes him an embittered man who has seen and succumbed to the ultimate force of doubt. The change that takes place at the end of "The Maypole of Merry Mount" is an imposed change, suffered by the Lord and Lady of the May when Endicott, a kind of reality principle, destroys the dream world of Merry Mount and carries them off into the darker but more real world of Puritanism. All of these transformations are symbolic, that is, they are pictures of real changes but do not really try to imitate the changes they signify. Our interest, in other words, is not in individuals; our attitude is not one of empathy with living characters. Hawthorne has succeeded in breaking through the more habitual drive of the imagination toward finding and empathizing with real characters, and he has planted a question. We do not so much feel what has happened as ask what it means. This is perhaps clearest in "The Gray Champion." He succeeds in routing the royalist army which confronts him and the Puritan crowd; but his action is prophetic action. He does not fight. He proclaims a truth and bears witness to it by symbolic gesture. The actual change is the political downfall of the King in England. It takes place outside the colony and is imposed upon it. The action within the story is symbolic, allegorical instead of mimetic.

It is possible now to draw these reflections on structure together in an attempt to say something about the structures which are typical of allegory. The discontinuous encounters which make up the stories of Robin Molineux and young Goodman Brown are cast in the form of journeys, geographical journeys on the surface, but psychological journeys in terms of meaning. Robin meets the representative forces of colonial-adult society one by one, and his symbolic encounters issue into his transformation at the end of the story. Young Goodman Brown meets the representatives of Puritan-adult society and his symbolic encounters issue into his own psychological and religious failure. Each story is unified by its drive toward a critical climax, but the material of its development is a series of encounters which we can recognize to be the fruit of a conceptual analysis either of social forces, as in "My Kinsman, Major Molineux," or of social types, as in "Young Goodman Brown." The story acquires, then, the rhythm of a ritual progress through what Hawthorne discovers to be the elemental confrontations of the adolescent with his particular society.

The other two stories are examples of a symmetrical stand-off of opposing forces. Each force is the representative of a certain concept about moral life, as in "The Maypole of Merry Mount"; or about government, as in "The Gray Champion." The development of "The Maypole of Merry Mount" was essentially an elaboration by means of ornamental imagery of the two hostile worlds of the dream and of reality. In "The Gray Champion" there is the same development of opposing forces; but in this case, as we have seen, the dialectic moves, acquires a certain suspense, and turns the story into a kind of battle. Still, it is not a battle, but a symbolic confrontation.

There are, then, two structures in our four allegories. According to Angus Fletcher in his chapter on symbolic action, progress and battle are the basic structures of allegory. They are because they are the basic structures of any presentation of concepts. One presents ideas in series, gradually building up their complexity, or one presents the conflict of ideas, either examining the two sides of a question or moving the question along in a pattern of statement and counter-statement. We will see the combination of both of these structural principles at work, though more subtly, in our examination of *The Scarlet Letter*.

Legends of the Province House

Hawthorne never succeeded in publishing his New England stories as a structural unit. His early effort, *Seven Tales of My Native Land,* seems to have gone into the fire because of despair over publication;[19] and a second effort, to be called *Provincial Tales,* was broken up for use in *The Token,* again for lack of a publisher to bring it out in book form.[20] Hawthorne continued to try grouping his stories into an overall structural unity with a third project to be called *The Story Teller*:

> A raconteur was to be represented as wandering over New England and regaling village audiences with his stories. Accounts of the storyteller's travels would provide homely, dramatic settings for the stories themselves.[21]

This final attempt to bring out a corpus of New England stories also failed; Park Benjamin, the editor of the *New England Magazine* "dropped out most of the connecting material,"[22] and Hawthorne's New England panorama never took shape. It has been left to the reader, then, to perceive the unity in Hawthorne's New England stories and to recognize that Hawthorne is exercising in them something of the function of public storyteller for his homeland.

If we look at the "Legends of the Province House" in the light of the whole panorama of New England as Hawthorne seems to have conceived it, we see how both thesis and antithesis were

continually at play in his allegorical imagination. We have seen
the worst of Puritanism in "Young Goodman Brown." We have
seen the brutality of American nationalism in "My Kinsman,
Major Molineux." We have seen the basic ambiguity of Hawthorne's attitude toward Puritanism in "The Gray Champion"
and especially in "The Maypole of Merry Mount." In the first
three of the "Legends of the Province House" we see the positive
side of Puritan-America, the rightness of the American cause;
but Hawthorne, true to himself, spins a fourth legend from the
heart of an old loyalist. By means of this shift of thematic view-
point, he is able, in spite of his American loyalties, to surround
the funeral of British rule in the American colonies with a certain aura of tragedy and loss. As Q. D. Leavis says, Hawthorne:

> felt that the significance of early America lay in the conflict
> between the Puritans who became New England and thus
> America, and the non-Puritans who were, to him, merely the
> English in America and whom he partly with triumph but
> partly also with anguish sees as being cast out. . . . He saw this
> process as a symbolic recurring struggle, an endless drama that
> he recorded in a series of works—*The Maypole, My Kinsman,
> Major Molineux, Endicott of the Red Cross, The Gray Cham-
> pion, The Scarlet Letter, The Blithedale Romance*, among
> others—that together form something that it would not be
> fanciful to˙ describe as a ritual drama reminding us of, for
> instance, the Norse Edda.[23]

Allegorical writing, we have seen, sacrifices the density of
realistic narrative and the human interest of realistic characterization in the interests of a clearer manipulation of a conceptual
theme. But Hawthorne has compensated for the flattening inherent in allegorical narrative by shifting the angle from which
the conceptual theme is viewed from story to story. We get a
sense of roundness, and fullness, of depth and authority which is
different from the fullness of mimetic fiction. The allegorical
form achieves its own authority in Hawthorne because he consistently examines all sides of his feeling for his native land.
Roundness and fullness, depth and authority come from looking
at the central concepts of New England religious and political
faith from all sides. The result, for a reader who reads Haw-

thorne's allegories of New England as an imaginative corpus, is
an intensification of interest in a fully realized thematic presentation, a specific pleasure attached to allegory as opposed to more
mimetic forms of plot and characterization. Though Hawthorne
writes as a patriot, he does not write as a propagandist. Though
he writes allegory, his allegory is open-ended, a research project
in American life rather than a body of conclusions.

In the "Legends of the Province House" the paragraphs of
historical essays are replaced by an overall narrative framework
consisting of the character of the narrator and a setting built up
from the kind of minute observation which characterizes large
passages of the American Notebooks. Still, the function per-
formed by the narrative framework is basically the same as that
of the historical essays: to set up some sort of continuity between
real present and legendary past.

At the opening of "Howe's Masquerade," Hawthorne literally
steps out of the present into a kind of readying room which is
not the past, but which stimulates Hawthorne's historical imagination and enables him to move freely in and out of the past:

> Entering the arched passage, which penetrated through the
> middle of a brick row of shops, a few steps transported me
> from the busy heart of modern Boston into a small and se-
> cluded courtyard. (952)

Once inside, much is made of the contrast between the barroom
of Hawthorne's day and its past glory as the center of government business, or between the cut-up chambers of Hawthorne's
day and the spacious chambers of the past. This movement back
and forth between the present lowliness and past glory of the
building is the way Hawthorne keeps his link with the past alive
and real. Counting on the vitality of this temporal lifeline, Hawthorne is free to endow the past with an aura of romance without fear of reducing it to fantasy and irrelevance.

Hawthorne, at the conclusion of all the Legends, describes
the atmosphere he has tried to create in order to free the imagination for its travels in the past:

> As the old loyalist concluded his narrative, the enthusiasm
> which had been fitfully flashing within his sunken eyes, and

quivering across his wrinkled visage, faded away, as if all the lingering fire of his soul were extinguished. Just then, too, a lamp upon the mantelpiece threw out a dying gleam, which vanished as speedily as it shot upward, compelling our eyes to grope for one another's features by the dim glow of the hearth. With such a lingering fire, methought, with such a dying gleam, had the glory of the ancient system vanished from the Province House, when the spirit of old Esther Dudley took its flight. And now, again, the clock of the Old South threw its voice of ages on the breeze, knolling the hourly knell of the Past, crying out far and wide through the multitudinous city, and filling our ears, as we sat in the dusky chamber, with its reverberating depth of tone. In that same mansion—in that very chamber—what a volume of history had been told off into hours, by the same voice that was now trembling in the air. Many a Governor had heard those midnight accents, and longed to exchange his stately cares for slumber. And as for mine host and Mr. Bela Tiffany and the old loyalist and me, we had babbled about dreams of the past, until we almost fancied that the clock was still striking in a bygone century. Neither of us would have wondered, had a hoop-petticoated phantom of Esther Dudley tottered into the chamber, walking her rounds in the hush of midnight, as of yore, and motioned us to quench the fading embers of the fire, and leave the historic precincts to herself and her kindred shades. (989)

Hawthorne shows us here how he has overcome the difficulty of writing romance about such a young, bright, and busy country as his own. The lights dim, as they always seem to do when Hawthorne moves away from the present. He uses this technique recurrently in the Legends. At the beginning of "Howe's Masquerade":

The panelled wainscot is covered with dingy paint, and acquires a duskier hue from the deep shadow into which the Province House is thrown by the brick block that shuts it in from Washington Street. A ray of sunshine never visits this apartment any more than the glare of the festal torches, which have been extinguished from the era of the Revolution. (952-953)

Again, in the introduction to "Edward Randolph's Portrait," Hawthorne dims the lights:

> Such a scene, dimly vanishing from the eye by the ray of here and there a tallow candle, glimmering through the small panes of scattered windows, would form a sombre contrast to the street as I beheld it, with the gaslights blazing from corner to corner, flaming within the shops, and throwing a noonday brightness through the huge plates of glass. (962-963)

The dying lights which illuminate the final scene of the "Legends of the Province House" are, then, the fitting conclusion for Hawthorne's extended stay in the past. Secondly, the Province House is haunted by the historical associations which Hawthorne complained of needing to bring his imagination into play. Finally, the vivid characterization of the old loyalist who tells the stories helps us measure the distance from Hawthorne's day into the past and makes us feel its reality by feeling the reality it has for this old man, in spite of the chill of antiquity. The old man is a kind of personification of the fictional power of memory and specifically, the memory of old times. The stories are about old dramas, old joys and old sorrows; but they come alive with a fiery energy which belies their distance in time. The vivid memories of a very real character, shaped into stories in the dim light of a history-haunted room, are what it takes to stimulate the imagination of Hawthorne and his readers. We will see this same set of circumstances perform the same function in "The Custom-House."

Howe's Masquerade

The creation of a kind of dream world, then, is not the technique of the "Legends of the Province House," as it was of "My Kinsman, Major Molineux," "Young Goodman Brown," and "The Maypole of Merry Mount." Our separation from the world

of daylight and reality took place rather as we passed with Hawthorne under the arch into the courtyard of the Province House.
But dream world or not, Hawthorne characteristically emphasizes the unreal in the description of the masquerade with which
he begins his narration:

> The brilliantly-lighted apartments were thronged with figures
> that seemed to have stepped from the dark canvas of historic
> portraits, or to have flitted forth from the magic pages of
> romance, or at least to have flown hither from one of the
> London theatres, without a change of garments. (954-955)

And this unreality is not merely a narrative technique for the
creation of romance, but rather, as in "The Maypole of Merry
Mount," has a thematic meaning: "It was the policy of Sir William Howe to hide the distress and danger of the period, and the
desperate aspect of the seige, under an ostentation of festivity"
(954). The masquerade is more than just fun; it is another
desperate attempt to escape the reality of the present anxiety,
and it is clearly doomed to the same failure as the deliberate
evasion of reality of the colonists of Merry Mount. A failure of
nerve before reality is Hawthorne's basic indictment of royalist
British rule.

The characters of "Howe's Masquerade," those, that is, who
create the action of the story by reacting to its pageant of historical figures, are Sir William Howe and Colonel Joliffe, who
as principal antagonists are seconded respectively by the Reverend Byles and Colonel Joliffe's granddaughter. All of them function typically as allegorical characters; they represent. Howe
represents British rule; Colonel Joliffe represents "the antique
spirit of his native land" (955). Howe's second is a somewhat
questionable member of the clergy, a group which was a frequent
target for Hawthorne's criticism: "if mirth were a crime, you had
never gained your doctorate in divinity" (955-956). The clergyman is infected, in other words, by a mirthful version of the
denial of reality which inspired Howe to hold his masquerade.
Colonel Joliffe's second, his granddaughter, complements the
Colonel's sobriety with her own wit and spirit.

In all four of these figures we have, again, conceptual meaning displacing rounded characterization, or rather we have human shapes given to two opposed and undeviating forces. Those qualities which seem to characterize them as individuals, Howe's bluster, Joliffe's severity, are seen on reflection to be rather qualities of the forces they represent: a blind pride on the part of the British, a stern determination on the part of the colonial American. *Force* is the proper word here, since both parties are presented, not as choosing but as possessed by antecedent wholehearted commitments. This is, as we have seen, typical both of Hawthorne and of allegorical characterization in general.

These, then, are the four characters of Hawthorne's allegory. But what they do in Hawthorne's allegory is observe and react to a second level of allegory. On this second level there are two rival and contending allegories. The first of these secondary allegories is Howe's masquerade itself. According to Robert H. Fossum, Howe and the British create a ludicrous allegory which mixes people of all historical periods into a mockery of the past.[24] Within this allegory, for example, a comic group of soldier-masquers under a scarecrow General Washington are mocked by a masquer dressed as the British Commander in Chief. But a second allegory, the procession of governors displaces the British allegory and shows that the British attempt to evade the lesson of the past is futile.

This second masque on the secondary level of allegory is composed of more purely allegorical figures. They are characterized not by action, but by decorative imagery. Each figure in the long procession of governors, is singled out by the use of costume and attributes: a rolled up banner of England rent and torn, along with a sword and a Bible for Endicott; a rolled manuscript for Winthrop, a stain of blood on the ruff of Sir Henry Vane; and so on throughout the long series of figures. This is an example of decorative imagery very much like that in "The Maypole of Merry Mount." Attributes and clothing indicate the personality of the wearer and place him in an over-arching order. This order is not a hierarchical order based on rank. Hawthorne's interest here is less in the hierarchical order of things than in the temporal order. The hierarchy created by time is the functioning order in his imagination.

Keeping in mind the fact that we have three allegories at work,

then, the basic allegorical opposition between Howe and Colonel
Joliffe, which *is* the story, and the allegories within the story,
the masquerade and the procession which displaces it and furnishes the subject matter to which the central protagonists react,
we see that the form of this third and dominant allegory is the
form of a ritual progress. There is no journey of a hero through
a series of adventures, as in "My Kinsman, Major Molineux" and
"Young Goodman Brown," but a journey of the mind down the
ages of history from governor to governor until an overwhelming
pattern of defeat and misery is established as the characteristic
of the reign of royal governors. The steady progress through past
governors leads inevitably to the climactic encounter in which
Howe beholds the figure of himself and sees the despairing gesture which he will one day inevitably make as he crosses the
threshold of the Province House.

If we step back, now, to the primary level of allegory, the confrontation between Howe and Colonel Joliffe, we can see that the
allegorical action on this level is not ritual progress but battle.
The battle turns out to be precisely a battle about how to react
to the forces of the past represented in the processional allegory.
Howe reacts with hostility, but also with impotence. A kind of
determinism possesses him. The unfolding pageant of triumphant
Puritan governors and agonizing British governors implies a kind
of predetermined historical drive in which Howe's personal choices
are fated. Hawthorne suggests that Howe is predestined to precisely the fate that he will meet.

> The martial shape again drew the cloak about his features and
> passed on; but reaching the threshold, with his back towards
> the spectators, he was seen to stamp his foot and shake his
> clinched hands in the air. It was afterwards affirmed that Sir
> William Howe had repeated that selfsame gesture of rage and
> sorrow, when, for the last time, and as the last royal governor,
> he passed through the portal of the Province House. (960)

Because he is what he is, an alien British ruler in a new world,
he is unable to see the lesson of history and so he is condemned
to be rendered helpless by it.[25] Colonel Joliffe, on the other hand,
becomes the guide and the interpreter of the historical procession.
These contrasting reactions continue throughout the procession,

interspersed with the reactions of others, until the victory is given to Colonel Joliffe. It is a symbolic victory, almost identical in nature with the victory of the Gray Champion. The implication is that Colonel Joliffe, or the American colonists, live realistically in the present and are consequently able to confront the past honestly and read it accurately.[26] The Americans are making history, says Hawthorne; and the British may try to evade it, but must submit to it in the end:

> Colonel Joliffe raised himself to the full height of his aged form, and smiled sternly on the British General.
> "Would your Excellency inquire further into the mystery of the pageant?" said he.
> "Take care of your gray head!" cried Sir William Howe, fiercely, though with a quivering lip. "It has stood too long on a traitor's shoulders!"
> "You must make haste to chop it off, then," calmly replied the Colonel; "for a few hours longer, and not all the power of Sir William Howe, nor of his master, shall cause one of these gray hairs to fall. The empire of Britain in this ancient province is at its last gasp tonight;—almost while I speak it is a dead corpse;—and methinks the shadows of the old governors are fit mourners at its funeral!" (961)

Talking about levels of allegory makes the story seem more complicated than it is. But if the whole comes off smoothly, it is because of Hawthorne's skill in manipulating allegorical levels. The basic allegory of the story is the confrontation between Howe and Colonel Joliffe. The two secondary allegories serve to echo or reflect this primary level. The secondary allegories are both rituals. They are so clearly distinct from the primary level because of this quality in them. Howe's own masquerade is a gathering of society into a kind of chaotic representation of the nature of British power in the colonies. In contrast to this there is a severe ritual rhythm to the third allegory, the procession which becomes the central structure of the story. The primary allegory then works itself out through opposed reactions to this central, though secondary allegory.

Hawthorne will do much the same thing in *The Scarlet Letter*. There too we will find social ritual to be the chief technique for bringing out the two allegorical levels of the story. There too the primary allegory will work itself out in terms of varying responses to the social rituals of Puritanism. There too he achieves a subtlety and interest which is altogether proper to meaning-centered as opposed to mimetic fiction, and which proves, by its emotional impact, that no apology need be advanced for Hawthorne's choice of the allegorical form for his fiction.

The suggestion of magic about the ritual procession deserves some notice. At the beginning, the narrator notes that the scene to be described "has never yet been satisfactorily explained" (954). When the first figure appears, "None could tell precisely from whence it came" (967). This sort of ambiguity is dropped during the presentation of the first three groups of governors. But with the dimming of the lights and the appearance of the fourth group, the ambiguous aura of magic begins once more to surround the scene. "Several figures, which passed hastily down the stairs and went forth from the porch, appeared rather like shadows than persons of fleshly substance" (959). When the final figure, the mimic representative of Sir William Howe himself, appears, the magic is more explicitly suggested:

A figure had come into view as if descending the stairs; although so dusky was the region whence it emerged, some of the spectators fancied that they had seen this human shape suddenly moulding itself amid the gloom. (960)

These are suggestions of magical causality. The real magic in the story, however, is seen in something we have noticed before as a kind of historical determinism. As the mimic figure departs, he makes exactly the gesture that Howe will make when he leaves the Province House. The connection between the mimic figure and Howe is left unexplained by Hawthorne. It is, in fact, both the unexplainable factor in the event and the factor which gives it meaning. Hawthorne leaves us with an impression of a mysterious connection between allegorical symbol and reality. This is all that Hawthorne does with magic in "Howe's Masquerade." It will be recognized that he plays with notions of magic throughout most of the stories he writes. We will see it, however, more fully exploited in "Lady Eleanore's Mantle." In this story magic is the sum and substance of the allegory, the basic technique by which the heavily moral lesson of the story is drawn.

Lady Eleanore's Mantle

The allegory in "Lady Eleanore's Mantle" is more explicit, perhaps even more traditional, than it is in any of the stories we have so far examined. It is not surprising, therefore, to find a more obvious use of the technical devices of allegory. To begin with characterization, we find Hawthorne so intent on bringing out the one dimension demanded by allegorical characterization that the realistic eye, which Hawthorne also keeps upon his characters, has to call them mad:

> Lady Eleanore was remarkable for a harsh, unyielding pride, a haughty consciousness of her hereditary and personal advantages, which made her almost incapable of control. Judging from many traditionary anecdotes, this peculiar temper was hardly less than a monomania; . . . . (972)

At her arrival Hawthorne presents her as the spirit incarnate of disaster: "Lady Eleanore Rochcliffe was ushered by a doleful clang, as if calamity had come embodied in her beautiful person" (973). When she draws her mantle about her at the ball, she gives "a completely new aspect to her beautiful face, which— half hidden, half revealed—seemed to belong to some being of mysterious character and purpose" (976). Finally, toward the end of the story, the anger of the people elicits the full suggestion that she is more than mad, she is demonic, the sexual partner of a fiend: "The people raved against the Lady Eleanore, and cried out that her pride and scorn had evoked a fiend, and that, between them both, this monstrous evil had been born" (978).

Lady Eleanore, the demonic representative of a virtually insane pride, requires a figure of the same conceptual purity to be the object of her scorn. She requires, that is, a madman to represent abjection as purely as she represents a mad pride. This figure is, of course, Jervase Helwyse. At Lady Eleanore's arrival Hawthorne is explicit about his two allegorical figures, bringing his story to a complete stop to interpret them:

> Then, though as lightly as a sunbeam on a cloud, she placed her foot upon the cowering form, and extended her hand to meet that of the governor. There was a brief interval, during which Lady Eleanore retained this attitude; and never, surely, was there an apter emblem of aristocracy and hereditary pride trampling on human sympathies and the kindred of nature, than these two figures presented at that moment. (973)

Jervase Helwyse, then, is also a pure symbol; and because of the purity of his representational function he too must appear, to the realistic eye, mad. It is the only way to make his actions in any way believable. But there is more to his madness than a technical requirement of allegory. We have seen that Jervase Helwyse is the representative of "human sympathies and the kindred of nature" which is the object of Lady Eleanore's scorn. Consequently, his own reaction to Lady Eleanore must tell us something about the reaction of common humanity to a pride such as Lady Eleanore's. His reaction, as we see in this first scene, is a kind of idolatry; and this idolatrous abjection before Lady Eleanore is true to his representational function. For the conclusion of the paragraph cited above reveals, among the people who witness the tableau, a deep sympathy with the abjection of Jervase Helwyse: "Yet the spectators were so smitten with her beauty, and so essential did pride seem to the existence of such a creature, that they gave a simultaneous acclamation of applause" (973). In the madness of Jervase Helwyse, Hawthorne makes us see the human tendency to let itself be trampled upon by the proud. The insight is repeated throughout the story. At the ball we recognize the human worship of the beautiful in the desperate wish of Jervase Helwyse to preserve the beauty of Lady Eleanore from the ruin to which it is fated. Finally, still the figure of common humanity's worship of proud beauty, Jervase Helwyse refuses to recognize, at the bedside of the plague-stricken Lady Eleanore, that such beauty could be subject to such ruin:

> "What thing art thou?" said the brain-stricken youth, drawing near the bed and tearing asunder its curtains. "Whose voice hast thou stolen for thy murmurs and miserable petitions, as

if Lady Eleanore could be conscious of mortal infirmity? Fie!
Head of diseased mortality, why lurkest thou in my lady's
chamber?" (980)

But once he has faced the fact, he turns upon the Lady Eleanore
all the hatred that the common man finds it in his heart to hurl
at the fallen, all the hatred his fascination would not allow him
to bestow on a triumphant pride: " 'Another triumph for the
Lady Eleanore!' he cried. 'All have been her victims! Who so
worthy to be the final victim as herself?' " (980) The madness
of Jervase Helwyse is, then, technically necessary to fit his actions
into a plausible narrative; but it is also thematically necessary to
make Jervase Helwyse a sign of the virtual madness which leads
common humanity to admire triumphant pride and to turn upon
pride when it has fallen into ruin.

With madness in control of the central characters of the story,
where is the voice of reason? Hawthorne, of course, intrudes
himself from time to time to point the moral of the story, but
there is also a bearer of the thematic burden within the story
itself. This is Dr. Clarke, who is marked, like Lady Eleanore
and Jervase Helwyse, with something beyond the human, but
whose power is the opposite of the malevolent power of madness:

> Looking fiercely up, with a madman's impulse to struggle with
> and rend asunder his opponent, he [Jervase Helwyse] found
> himself powerless beneath a calm, stern eye, which possessed
> the mysterious property of quelling frenzy at its height. The
> person whom he had now encountered was the physician,
> Doctor Clarke, ... (979)

Possessed of a firmer and saner power, Dr. Clarke is able to act
as the representative of a kind of wisdom which is above both
monomaniacal pride and the stupefied abjection of common man.
It is he who speaks up in defense of the rights of common man:

> "With your pardon, sir," replied Doctor Clarke, . . . "what-
> ever the heralds may pretend, a dead beggar must have prece-
> dence of a living queen. King Death confers high privileges."
> (973)

Although Hawthorne's democratic sympathies are strong, he has
no illusions about the wisdom of common humanity. Faced with

the arrogance of pure pride, man falls down and worships:

> "Poor youth!" said Doctor Clarke; and, moved by a deep sense
> of human weakness, a smile of caustic humor curled his lip
> even then. "Wilt thou still worship the destroyer and surround
> her image with fantasies the more magnificent, the more evil
> she has wrought? Thus man doth ever to his tyrants. . ." (979)

It takes a wise man who stands apart from it all to take up the
defense of humanity and its rights.

The character of Dr. Clarke is the most developed example
so far of the allegorical guide. We have seen the suggestion of
a guide in the latter part of "My Kinsman, Major Molineux";
a satanic guide in "Young Goodman Brown"; and a rather
schematically employed guide in Colonel Joliffe. Here Hawthorne
has employed the guide figure almost as a second omniscient
narrator within the action of the story. Dr. Clarke knows, for no
plausible reason other than his function in the allegory, the background of Jervase Helwyse's madness: "it was his misfortune
to meet this Lady Eleanore Rochcliffe. He loved her—and her
scorn has driven him mad" (974). He interprets in advance the
events which are to come:

> "It may be so," said Doctor Clarke, frowning as he spoke.
> "But I tell you, sir, I could well-nigh doubt the justice of
> Heaven above us if no signal humiliation overtake this lady,
> who now treads so haughtily into yonder mansion. She seeks
> to place herself above the sympathies of our common nature,
> which envelops all human souls. See, if that nature do not
> assert its claim over her in some mode that shall bring her
> level with the lowest!" (974)

At the ball, he furnishes the needed insight into the connection
between Lady Eleanore and the plague: "Woe to those who shall
be smitten by this beautiful Lady Eleanore!" (977).

The doctor's strange power over Jervase Helwyse leads us to
the question of "power" in general within "Lady Eleanore's
Mantle." The doctor is a kind of scientist, and Hawthorne clearly
means that fact to be part of the explanation of his powers. But
he also means the doctor's power to be beyond science, and this
suggests that Hawthorne deals in another type of power over

nature than the scientist's. This second power is the power of magic.[27] We find, upon examination, that just as "Lady Eleanore's Mantle" is the most allegorical of these stories, so is it the most thoroughly founded upon magic, the causality principle proper to allegory.

Hawthorne's problem in constructing the story was to build and maintain a causal nexus between Lady Eleanore's pride and the ravages of the plague. Hawthorne eventually gives an acceptably realistic causal explanation of the contagion: The infection is traced back to Lady Eleanore, to her mantle, and finally to the diseased and dying woman who had embroidered it. But Hawthorne is not really interested in plausibility. He is interested in allegorical significance, in making a story about the ravages of pride. Consequently, before he clarifies his realistic causal series, he insists that we recognize and accept a more mysterious linkage in the chain of events. To get the meaning of the story we must accept the allegorical convention of a magical connection between a physical disease and a moral one. The mantle, then, as the symbol of Lady Eleanore's pride, is given magical power:

A singular tale had gone abroad among the ladies of the province, that their fair rival was indebted for much of the irresistible charm of her appearance to a certain article of dress—an embroidered mantle—which had been wrought by the most skilful artist in London, and possessed even magical properties of adornment. (972)

The initial impression of benevolent magical power is a false lead. At the ball Hawthorne begins to suggest a malevolent latency in the mantle:

Wild fancy as it is, this mysterious mantle has thrown an awe around my image of her, partly from its fabled virtues, and partly because it was the handiwork of a dying woman, and, perchance, owed the fantastic grace of its conception to the delirium of approaching death. (975)

Finally, toward the end of the story, we are told:

There remained no room for doubt that the contagion had lurked in that gorgeous mantle, which threw so strange a grace

around her at the festival. Its fantastic splendor had been conceived in the delirious brain of a woman on her deathbed, and
was the last toil of her stiffening fingers, which had interwoven
fate and misery with its golden threads. (978)

By this time the allegorical significance of the mantle has been
so elaborated as to make the natural explanation of its contagion
unimportant. All the emphasis is on the pride of the Lady
Eleanore who wore the mantle:

> It had been traced back to a lady's luxurious chamber—to the
> proudest of the proud—to her that was so delicate, and hardly
> owned herself of earthly mould—to the haughty one, who took
> her stand above human sympathies—to Lady Eleanore! (978)

There is a larger context for the magical power at work within
this story than simply the allegorical convention adopted for the
purposes of the story. Hawthorne says, at the beginning of his
narrative, that "it seemed due from Providence that pride so
sinful should be followed by as severe a retribution" (972). Is
it far-fetched to call the Puritan belief in Providence magical?
Belief in providence is not itself, of course, either superstitious
or magical. But the Puritan notion of a providence which re-
dresses the balance of wrongs on this earth was a primitive belief,
without the excuse of primitive times. Even in Old Testament
times theology had developed far beyond such thinking. A more
sophisticated understanding of providence recognizes its trans-
cendence. God's way of ruling the world is lost in mystery, and
Christian revelation claims to be at most but a partial glimpse
into the mystery. The Puritans vulgarized providence to bring it
within the range of everyman's power of interpretation—as Puritan diaries abundantly illustrate. Such an anthropomorphic conception of providence is superstitious, reductively magical. Hawthorne is the skeptical heir of this tradition of belief. He uses
providence as the religious mask for a fundamentally magical
allegorical setting in which the plague can be linked as punishment to pride; but he does so with a kind of apology which indicates his sense of the fact that he is employing a religious belief
as a literary technique:

> That tinge of the marvellous, which is thrown over so many
> of these half-forgotten legends, has probably imparted an

additional wildness to the strange story of Lady Eleanore Rochcliffe. (972)

The pride of Lady Eleanore is "a haughty consciousness of her hereditary and personal advantages" (972). It is the pride of an aristocrat, and aristocracy is the social form of the pride that Hawthorne's allegory attacks.[28] The contrast between aristocracy and common humanity is made clear from the first. At the moment of Lady Eleanore's arrival a young British captain is incensed that a funeral bell should be tolling. We have seen Dr. Clarke's response: "a dead beggar must have precedence of a living queen" (973). Hawthorne uses the ball to elaborate the contrast. As we saw in "Howe's Masquerade," a ball is a social ritual that says something about the society which gathers for it. It is as significant as the mob scene in "My Kinsman, Major Molineux," the gathering of the witches in "Young Goodman Brown," the dance at Merry Mount. Here the decoration fulfills again the allegorical roles of signalizing rank and passing judgment:

> The ladies shone in rich silks and satins, outspread over wide-projecting hoops; and the gentlemen glittered in gold embroidery, laid unsparingly upon the purple, or scarlet, or sky-blue velvet, which was the material of their coats and waistcoats. The latter article of dress was of great importance, since it enveloped the wearer's body nearly to the knees, and was perhaps bedizened with the amount of his whole year's income, in golden flowers and foliage. (974)

Hawthorne does not take the existence of an aristocracy for granted, as would an allegorist still writing under the dominant belief in a stable, hierarchic society. Hawthorne employs the symbols of rank to criticize rank:

> The altered taste of the present day—a taste symbolic of a deep change in the whole system of society—would look upon almost any of those gorgeous figures as ridiculous; although that evening the guests sought their reflections in the pier-glasses, and rejoiced to catch their own glitter amid the glittering crowd. (974)

The criticism here is from a historical perspective. Hawthorne furnishes his aristocracy with the splendor of rank not only to set them off vertically from the common people, but also and especially to set them off horizontally from the transformed society of Hawthorne's day:

> What a pity that one of the stately mirrors has not preserved a picture of the scene, which, by the very traits that were so transitory, might have taught us much that would be worth knowing and remembering! (974)

Both of these "hierarchical" perspectives are necessary to the allegory of "Lady Eleanore's Mantle" because Hawthorne is not saying that within the hierarchical structure those who possess high rank should not violate the chain of humanity. Rather the institution of aristocracy itself is a violation of the chain of humanity. Consequently the plague will be linked not only to the pride of Lady Eleanore, but to the pride of the whole aristocratic system of which she is meant to be a radical type.

Hawthorne shows us how the circle of those who surround Lady Eleanore at the ball contracts, setting up that isolation which will eventually point her out as the source of the plague, "Gradually, Lady Eleanore Rochcliffe's circle grew smaller, till only four gentlemen remained in it" (975). These four figures outline the social classes which share in her aristocracy. The English military officer; the Virginia planter, an American aristocrat; the Episcopal clergyman, representative of royalist religion; and the private secretary of Governor Shute, a member of the royal government; all of them are representatives of an aristocratic world which is trying to impose itself on the primitive democracy of New England. The contagion will work its way out from the Lady Eleanore and these four aristocratic figures, following a path already prepared for it by their social sin of pride. That this is not a natural course for the plague to follow, Hawthorne is careful to point out:

> At first, unlike its ordinary course, the disease seemed to confine itself to the higher circles of society, selecting its victims from among the proud, the well-born, and the wealthy, entering unabashed into stately chambers, and lying down with the slumberers in silken beds. (977)

Hawthorne is rarely satisfied with a less than social theme.

Lady Eleanore's sin is isolation from the chain of human sympathies; this is both stated and symbolized in her refusal to participate in the refreshments at the ball. But her first refusal of human communion is given religious overtones by her symbolically charged refusal at the climax of the ball. Jervase Helwyse appears at her feet with the sacramental vessels of the Eucharist, "which he offered as reverentially as to a crowned queen, or rather with the awful devotion of a priest doing sacrifice to his idol" (975-976). What he asks of Lady Eleanore is an explicit sacramental act of communion:

I pray you to take one sip of this holy wine, and then to pass the goblet round among the guests. And this shall be a symbol that you have not sought to withdraw yourself from the chain of human sympathies. . . . (976)

A sacramental action in the Christian faith is an encounter with Christ. Through that charity-building encounter the act becomes an act of communion with the Christian community. Here, of course, there is no truly sacramental encounter, but an attempt to use the symbols of such an encounter to create an aura of religious significance. The religious significance, however, has the same value as the notion of providence we have discussed. The act is basically an attempt to cure the disease of isolation and pride by a symbolic act with no other base than magic. The disease, of course, will find its cure, but in a disastrous way. The plague will create first a massive fragmentation of society. Men will be cut off from one another by fear of contagion. Only their common desperation will bring them together, and then only because social hierarchies, the isolating structures built by pride, will have crumbled before the common human condition.

But the disease, pursuing its onward progress, soon ceased to be exclusively a prerogative of aristocracy. Its red brand was no longer conferred like a noble's star, or an order of knighthood. It threaded its way through the narrow and crooked streets, and entered the low, mean, darksome dwellings, and laid its hand of death upon the artisans and laboring classes of the town. It compelled rich and poor to feel themselves brethren then; . . . . (978)

Hawthorne uses the sacramental vessels and the act of communion to heighten the climax of his story. He chose the mantle, however, as his central symbol; and so he links the mantle to the sacramental symbols by having the contents of the chalice spill upon the mantle. This is a kind of desecration of the sacrament, and the suggestion, which is characteristic of a magical notion of sacramental power, is that a desecrated sacrament has a malevolent effect.

Pride has rejected human communion, and the direct result, within the allegorical world Hawthorne has created, is the plague. The red flag which now appears as the symbol of the triumph of pride becomes the symbol of Lady Eleanore's triumph until Jervase Helwyse takes over as the banner-bearer of the plague. Just as the plague is magically connected as punishment to the pride of aristocracy, so it is magically destroyed when Jervase Helwyse, the representative of abject humanity sinned against by pride, leads the ritual procession which terminates in the burning of the mantle. Magical causality is the underlying supposition upon which rests the whole action of the story.

We have seen some of the basic techniques of allegory employed in stories by Hawthorne that are both historical and allegorical. For Hawthorne the historical was the favored realm of the allegorical, something else that we shall see better in examining *The Scarlet Letter*. Before going on to that work, however, there are two paradoxical qualities about Hawthorne's allegories which give us an insight into that which is particular to him in his use of the form. Allegorical imagery is, according to Angus Fletcher, concerned with establishing or illustrating a hierarchy of social ranks. In Hawthorne, however, social differentiation into higher and lower ranks is considered a violation of the community of human sympathy. Secondly, allegory tends to create a dream world, or, if not that, a type of never-never land in which the requirements of reality are slackened to allow for the action of figures governed by their conceptual significance. But in Hawthorne, the tendency to surround or infuse the real world with fantasy, such as is done by the colonists of Merry Mount, is itself a target against which the allegory is directed. Hawthorne is an allegorist who uses the techniques of the form to attack one of its basic imaginative requirements. As we continue our analysis of

Hawthorne's allegory in *The Scarlet Letter* we will find that Hawthorne uses the literary form of allegory with devastating accuracy against the whole tradition of thought, exemplified in an extreme way by Puritanism, which tries to control reality by imposing an allegorical interpretation on it.

NOTES

[1] The various levels of the allegory as interpreted by Q. D. Leavis, Hyatt Howe Waggoner, and Roy R. Male are all included in Daniel G. Hoffman's "Yankee Bumpkin and Scapegoat King," Chapter 6 of *Form and Fable in American Fiction* (New York: Oxford University Press, 1961), pp. 113-125. Arthur T. Broes, "Journey into Moral Darkness: 'My Kinsman, Major Molineux' as Allegory," *NCF* 19 (Sept., 1964), 171-184, also summarizes interpretations and complains that the relationship of the story to earlier allegories, especially Spenser's and Bunyan's, has been neglected. Only Thomas E. Connors, " 'My Kinsman, Major Molineux': A Reading," *MLN* 74 (April, 1959), 229-302, denies that the tale is allegorical. It is, rather, a "brutally realistic account of human viciousness."

[2] Page references in parentheses after citations from the tales are to *The Complete Novels and Selected Tales of Nathaniel Hawthorne*, edited by Norman Holmes Pearson (New York: The Modern Library, 1937).

[3] Seymour L. Gross, "Hawthorne's 'My Kinsman, Major Molineux': History as Moral Adventure," *NCF* 12 (Sept. 1957), 99.

[4] F. O. Matthiessen, *American Renaissance* (New York: Oxford University Press, 1941), p. 266.

[5] See Terence Martin, *The Instructed Vision: Scottish Common Sense Philosophy and the Origins of American Fiction* (Bloomington: Indiana University Press, 1961).

[6] *The Old Glory* (New York: Farrar, Straus and Giroux, 1965), p. 66.

[7] Honig, *op. cit.,* p. 68. John Burrow, "Allegory: The Literal Level," a lecture given at Yale University, Oct. 2, 1967, finds three phases in the history of the allegorical surface: (1) Neo-medieval: the meaning is all; the surface may be incoherent; (2) Neo-classical: the surface must be coherent as well as a reflection of the meaning beyond the surface; (3) Neo-romantic compromise: the coherence of the surface is not that of everyday mimetic reality, but that of dream.

[8] Q. D. Leavis, "Hawthorne as Poet," *Sewanee Review* 59 (Spring and Summer, 1951), 179-205, 426-458, cited in *Interpretations of American Literature,* edited by Charles Feidelson, Jr., and Paul Brodtkorb, Jr. ("A Galaxy Book," paper; New York: Oxford University Press, 1959), p. 45.

[9] *Op. cit.,* pp. 12-13.

[10] Honig, *op. cit.,* p. 5: "A good allegory, like a good poem, does not exhibit devices or hammer away at intentions. It beguiles the reader with a continuous interplay between subject and sense in the storytelling, and the narrative, the story itself, means everything."

[11] Fletcher, *op. cit.,* p. 66.

[12] Honig, *op. cit.,* p. 78.

[13] Honig, *op. cit.*, p. 197, n. 7.

[14] *The Sins of the Fathers: Hawthorne's Psychological Themes* (New York: Oxford University Press, 1966), pp. 28-29. Hoffman, *op. cit.*, who sees the importance of the specific historical setting of "Young Goodman Brown" to the meaning, does not see it here, p. 144: "Hawthorne's major theme is neither the supersession of religions nor of cultures; what he does here dramatize is the evolution of self-knowledge in the human soul."

[15] *Op. cit.*, p. 17.

[16] *Op. cit.*, p. 36.

[17] In a classroom presentation at Yale in the fall of 1963.

[18] *Op. cit.*, p. 40.

[19] N. F. Adkins, "The Early Projected Works of Nathaniel Hawthorne," *PBSA* 39 (Second Quarter, 1945), 127-131.

[20] Randall Stewart, *Nathaniel Hawthorne: A Biography* (paper, New Haven: Yale University Press, 1948), pp. 29-30.

[21] *Ibid.*, p. 31.

[22] *Ibid.*, p. 32.

[23] *Op. cit.*, p. 35.

[24] "Time and the Artist in 'Legends of the Province House,' " *NCF* 21 (March, 1967), 337-348.

[25] *Ibid.*

[26] *Ibid.*

[27] Hawthorne infuses science with a quality of magic in the character of Chillingworth in *The Scarlet Letter*. There, of course, both science and magical power are malevolent. For a discussion of this whole question see Elizabeth Ruth Hosmer. *Science and Pseudo-Science in the Writing of Nathaniel Hawthorne* (Urbana: 1950).

[28] See Seymour L. Gross, "Hawthorne's 'Lady Eleanore's Mantle' as History," *JEGP* 54 (1955), 549-554.

The Custom House

Unity

The fact that the story of *The Scarlet Letter* seems to have no intrinsic dependence on its introductory essay has caused many critics to reject it, among them, W. C. Brownell,[1] Austin Warren,[2] and Edward Wagenknecht.[3] But there is an increasing body of criticism which finds that "The Custom-House" adds important dimensions to the whole. Charles Feidelson, in *Symbolism and American Literature,* binds the two parts of the fictional structure together with an epistemological theme: how a symbol acquires meaning. In "The Custom-House" we see Hawthorne absorbed in the contemplation of the letter. In the story proper each character re-enacts Hawthorne's contemplation in his own way and with his own results.[4] It seems necessary, however, to add to this epistemological concern a moral and psychological concern which is more central to the experience of the novel. Hawthorne is interested in the problem of meaning because the way the Puritans solved the problem was frightening in its destructive potentialities.[5] For Earl H. Rovit, who is also convinced that the problem of meaning is the central problem, the hero of the story is Hawthorne—a logical corollary of this position. Rovit then pushes on to the moral and psychological aspects of the problem of meaning. What he finds is an unresolved dilemma.

If these characters [of The Scarlet Letter] did not try to impose a pattern on their lives, they would succumb to the torpor of Death-in-life—they would be one with Hawthorne's sluggardly old sea captains in the Custom-House. But, ironically, when they do make such a creative effort, they are trapped in the

61

absurdity of a self-imposed design and they put to death the
infinite possibilities of their individual existences.[6]

It seems to me that there are positive values to be found in *The
Scarlet Letter,* however, which escape this sort of ambiguity, even
though none of the characters within the novel may be the representative of those positive values. Other critics who have addressed
themselves to the problem of the unity of preface and story have
brought out parallels between Hawthorne and Dimmesdale and
Hawthorne and Hester, as well as contrasts between Hawthorne's
Custom-House milieu and Puritan times. The present analysis is
an attempt to show how all of these insights into the unity of
Hawthorne's work are rooted in the literary form of allegory as
Hawthorne recreated it. To return to the allegorical tradition,
what do we see when we regard "The Custom-House" as a
prefatory statement-of-intention like the traditional prefaces to
the allegories of Spenser and Bunyan?

Traditional Prefaces

Hawthorne himself throws us off the track by disclaiming any
structural function for "The Custom-House." He refers to his
earlier "autobiographical impulse," the one which inspired "The
Old Manse," as inexcusable. He had given in to that impulse
"for no earthly reason, that either the indulgent reader or the
intrusive author could imagine" (3).[7] The only reason "The
Custom-House" is being written, then, is that "beyond my deserts,
I was happy enough to find a listener or two on the former occasion" (3). In other words, this essay is as irrelevant to the fiction
of *The Scarlet Letter* as that one was to the looser structure of
Mosses from an Old Manse. But Hawthorne's modest authorial
disclaimers and surface apologies are not to be trusted any more
than his claim to be merely the editor of the story of *The Scarlet
Letter.* The relationships among writer, reader, and work had
changed since the times of Spenser and Bunyan. The element of
irony in Hawthorne's prefaces is not merely an expression of his

own ironic and skeptical personality. It is, as we shall see, a result
of the change in the fictional situation. We must do the best we
can to infer Hawthorne's intentions, since we cannot expect him
to state them. Not only "The Custom-House" but the earlier essay,
"The Old Manse," to which Hawthorne alludes as a parallel
instance of "the autobiographical impulse," give us the little evidence we have about what Hawthorne wanted to do in writing
The Scarlet Letter.

What we find in both "The Old Manse" and "The Custom-
House" is an author who is less sure of the social importance of
his authorship than were Spenser and Bunyan. He measures himself and his literary work against the activities of men who have,
or have had, a recognized place in American society. We see
then, in spite of the irony, how important Hawthorne felt it to be
to establish the importance of his fiction against the imagined
condemnation of his Puritan ancestors. To him, for all his playful
modesty, his stories were anything but "toys." The later opinion
of Henry James that they were toys,[8] and that Hawthorne was
mischievously in agreement with his Puritan forebears has its
truth. All stories are toys in so far as they are not tools. James
supposes too great a distance between play and moral concern.
Hawthorne's playing is very serious, as most criticism since James
has recognized.

In "The Old Manse" Hawthorne tells us with ironic delight
how inspiring a place the old parsonage was for a writer. It is
"awful to reflect how many sermons must have been written
there" (374);[9] and so Hawthorne takes shame to himself for
"having been so long a writer of idle stories," and resolves "at
least to achieve a novel that should evolve some deep lesson and
should possess physical substance enough to stand alone." The
irony here is not, it seems to me, directed at the kind of novel he
claims to want to write, but rather at himself for not having
written it by the time his stay at the Old Manse was over. Through
the irony we see that his sense of what it is to write a story
includes a strong bias toward the didactic.

Later in "The Old Manse," after taking his readers on a
leisurely tour of the river, the garden, the orchards, where nature's
fertility is so strongly felt, Hawthorne returns to the dusty writings
of the library with a reinforced sense of their sterility.

The rain pattered upon the roof and the sky gloomed through the dusty garret windows, while I burrowed among these venerable books in search of any living thought which should burn like a coal of fire, or glow like an inextinguishable gem, beneath the dead trumpery that had long hidden it. But I found no such treasure; all was dead alike; and I could not but muse deeply and wonderingly upon the humiliating fact that the works of man's intellect decay like those of his hands. Thought grows mouldy. What was good and nourishing food for the spirits of one generation affords no sustenance for the next. Books of religion, however, cannot be considered a fair test of the enduring and vivacious properties of human thought, because such books so seldom really touch upon their ostensible subject, and have, therefore, so little business to be written at all. So long as an unlettered soul can attain to saving grace, there would seem to be no deadly error in holding theological libraries to be accumulations of, for the most part, stupendous impertinence. (387)

Hawthorne's emphasis seems to indicate that he knew himself to be saying what was not generally accepted in the world of his time. He was, then, aware of the actual challenge which such a body of outdated writing presented, in spite of the fact that he himself was perfectly aware of its impertinence. Obviously, then, he is holding out the possibility that another kind of writing will surmount the danger of such impertinence.

There is another kind of writing, or at least of literary activity, in the environs of the Old Manse. Hawthorne's most immediate dialogue with Transcendentalism was carried on through the friendship of Ellery Channing. But that gathering of thinkers who were attracted by the widespread influence of Emerson, attained "just so much of insight . . . as to make life all a labyrinth" (397). Hawthorne "admired Emerson as a poet of deep beauty and austere tenderness, but sought nothing from him as a philosopher" (397). Hawthorne produced no philosophy, then, but only "idle weeds and withering blossoms" (400).

The treasure of intellectual good which I hoped to find in our secluded dwelling had never come to light. No profound treatise of ethics, no philosophic history, no novel even, that could stand unsupported on its edges. All that I had to show, as a man of letters, were these few tales and essays, which had blossomed out like flowers in the calm summer of my heart and mind. (400)

Although Hawthorne rejected the sterile world of theological discourse and failed to be touched by the burgeoning world of transcendental philosophy, he shares with these traditions the desire to produce work of a certain ethical substance.

Hawthorne's kinship with these two traditions and his proximity to the days when truth was almost exclusively conveyed by means of preaching, occasions a reflection on a remark of Edwin Honig about the early days of Greek literature. Honig remarks that there is a relationship between the early allegorical interpreters of Homer and primitive religion:

> Hence, the interpreter, as we may envisage him in the sixth century B.C., is identified with an earlier privileged class of guardians, primitive fathers, heroes, and gods. Like them he seeks to preserve the images of authority and the transcendence of cultural principles.[10]

Granting, of course, the long literary history which separates Hawthorne from those early literary men and the fact that they interpreted while Hawthorne created, there still seems to be a significant parallel between Greek literature and philosophy emerging from its matrix in primitive religion and American literature emerging from its matrix in the New England Puritan milieu. This explains why Hawthorne seems less concerned to continue a fictional tradition and more concerned to elevate or re-cast the homiletic tradition. It is against this homiletic tradition —continued in the sermon-lecture of the transcendentalists—that he measures his own literary output. Hawthorne never takes over from the dying Puritan priesthood the role of preserver of cultural values. But in many of his sketches and stories he does test them, and with a touch of irony of which both Puritanism and Transcendentalism were incapable.

In "The Old Manse," then, we see an author of fiction measuring himself against men who philosophized and men who wrote sermons, and we perceive a concern to do in his fiction what failed to be done in those old sermons, and what he probably felt failed to be done as well by the philosophers in spite of their much touted free play of the intellect.

When we return to "The Custom-House," we find Hawthorne measuring himself against a different kind of man. In this world of government functionaries neither books nor nature, the two founts of spiritual existence, had any importance; and so, of course, he recognized that his own literary achievements were totally without significance to his colleagues. He chuckled ironically at the thought that now his name was being spread throughout the world, not on title-pages, but imprinted

> with a stencil and black paint, on pepper-bags and baskets of anatto, and cigar-boxes, and bales of all kinds of dutiable merchandise, in testimony that these commodities had paid the impost, and gone regularly through the office. (27)

Here, too, in the Custom-House, a vast amount of futile writing had been produced:

> It was sorrowful to think how many days, and weeks, and months, and years of toil, had been wasted on these musty papers, which were now only an encumbrance on earth, and were hidden away in this forgotten corner, never more to be glanced at by human eyes. (28)

The parallel between these writings and the Puritan sermons in the library of the Old Manse is obvious.

Finally, however, Hawthorne has to face the ultimate unpleasant fact. It is not only Puritan sermons, Transcendental musings, and these official records which elicit a sense of futility:

> But, then, what reams of other manuscripts—filled, not with the dulness of official formalities, but with the thought of inventive brains and the rich effusion of deep hearts—had gone equally to oblivion; and that, moreover, without serving a purpose in their day, as these heaped-up papers had, and— saddest of all—without purchasing for their writers the comfortable livelihood which the clerks of the Custom-House had gained by these worthless scratchings of the pen. (28)

Even the products of the would-be artist's imaginative efforts must eventually be called into question. The risk of being a writer is the risk of total failure, of total obscurity, of the loss not only of present or future fame, but of the present satisfaction of gaining a livelihood for himself and his family. Yet Hawthorne clearly sees that risk and takes it, another suggestion of how basic was his commitment as an artist. In the light of such self-questioning, it is no wonder that an author who accepts the risk of writing should himself be the real hero who is put through his trial by ordeal in the very act of writing his story.

There was, however, in the midst of so much futility, a kind of "successful" writing which acted as a siren call luring Hawthorne, throughout most of his life, away from the kind of writing which was most proper to his genius. In the library of the Old Manse he had discovered some writings which seemed to have retained their vitality over the span of years.

> There were a few old newspapers, and still older almanacs, which reproduced to my mental eye the epochs when they had issued from the press with a distinctness that was altogether unaccountable. It was as if I had found bits of magic looking-glass among the books, with the images of a vanished century in them. I turned my eyes towards the tattered picture above mentioned, and asked of the austere divine wherefore it was that he and his brethren, after the most painful rummaging and groping into their minds, had been able to produce nothing half so real as these newspaper scribblers and almanac makers had thrown off in the effervescence of a moment. (388)

Reflecting upon these ephemera, he sees the link between them and genius:

> It is the age itself that writes newspapers and almanacs, which, therefore, have a distinct purpose and meaning at the time, and a kind of intelligible truth for all times; whereas most other works—being written by men who, in the very act, set themselves apart from their age—are likely to possess little significance when new, and none at all when old. Genius, indeed, melts many ages into one, and thus effects something permanent, yet still with a similarity of office to that of the more ephemeral writer. A work of genius is but the newspaper of a century, or perchance of a hundred centuries. (388)

Accordingly, in "The Custom-House" Hawthorne reflects that the writer who penetrates the hard surface of contemporary fact chooses the surer way to creating a work of genius:

> It was a folly, with the materiality of this daily life pressing so intrusively upon me, to attempt to fling myself back into another age; or to insist on creating the semblance of a world out of airy matter, when, at every moment, the impalpable beauty of my soap-bubble was broken by the rude contact of some actual circumstance. The wiser effort would have been, to diffuse thought and imagination through the opaque substance of to-day, and thus to make it a bright transparency; to spiritualize the burden that began to weigh so heavily; to seek, resolutely, the true and indestructible value that lay hidden in the petty and wearisome incidents, and ordinary characters, with which I was now conversant. The fault was mine. The page of life that was spread out before me seemed dull and commonplace, only because I had not fathomed its deeper import. A better book than I shall ever write was there; . . . . (37)

"Blasted allegories" is what Hawthorne, in a letter to Fields in 1854, called his writing; but Jesse Bier has warned us against taking Hawthorne's self-deprecation about his allegorical writing too seriously:

> His self-critical "inveterate love for allegory" cannot be taken at face value, for the technique of the allegory was one of the highest expressions of the imagination to Hawthorne.[11]

He does not actually apologize for how he writes. Rather he seems simply to doubt that the allegorical form is an effective way of doing what other forms had failed to do. Edwin Honig seems to touch upon the roots of this uncertainty:

> Hawthorne's prefaces seem more objective than either Spenser's or Bunyan's; actually they are more personal and recognize an essential difficulty that accompanies his reformulation of the allegorical method inherited from Bunyan and Spenser.[12]

Hawthorne was convinced of the value of realism, but equally convinced of the difficulties that realistic writing created for him.

So he was faced with the problem of writing allegory in a world which continued to produce masses of written material, all of which was almost immediately impertinent and unreadable, except for the realistic flashes of journalism. It is no wonder that he was uncertain, having, as he did, to shape allegory anew in a world whose literature had dried up.

There is one final group, a crucial one, against which Hawthorne must measure himself. These are his own Puritan ancestors:

> The figure of that first ancestor, invested by family tradition with a dim and dusky grandeur, was present to my boyish imagination, as far back as I can remember. It still haunts me, and induces a sort of home-feeling with the past, ... (9)

It is this ancestry which weds him to Salem and gives him an identity there:

> I seem to have a stronger claim to a residence here on account of this grave, bearded, sable-cloaked, and steeple-crowned progenitor,—who came so early, with his Bible and his sword, and trode the unworn street with such a stately port, and made so large a figure, as a man of war and peace,—a stronger claim than for myself, whose name is seldom heard and my face hardly known. (9)

Yet these people would be bound to reject him and his aims:

> No aim, that I have ever cherished, would they recognize as laudable; no success of mine—if my life, beyond its domestic scope, had ever been brightened by success—would they deem otherwise than worthless, if not positively disgraceful. (10)

Still, he is bound to admit their influence on him: "Let them scorn me as they will, strong traits of their nature have intertwined themselves with mine" (10). Those traits are to be found in Hawthorne precisely as a creator of fiction. He has the seriousness of his Puritan forebears, the driving conscience which impels him on in spite of the fact that he has rejected so much of what they stood for. He is, in other words, a Puritan transformed into a writer of fiction.[13]

His sense of mission is strong in spite of his irony. Consequently, though he was not cast down by the imagined condemnation of these long dead ancestors, he had enough of their
dedication to his vocation to be cast down at the thought of
losing his sensitivity and creative power while stagnating as a
surveyor in the Custom-House. As a true child of his fathers he
could not bear that what he did there was "of no advantage nor
delight to any human being" (42). He had the Puritan's "unquiet
impulse" that had to be stilled by giving himself to his "toil."

Hawthorne, then, does not write a traditional preface to a traditional allegory to tell us what he intends to do. Rather, in the
course of the two prefatory essays, "The Old Manse" and "The
Custom-House" he asks all the questions an author can ask of
himself about the significance of his writing. His answers do not
orchestrate a resounding affirmation of the importance of his
work. He leaves us to judge that for ourselves. All he will say
is that he is laying himself on the line, and doing so with a full
awareness of his own serious commitment. He will say something
significant, in spite of all that may be adduced by himself or by
others against that possibility.

The Four Phases

Hawthorne develops the Custom-House essay in four phases
which, though they interpenetrate, remain more or less distinct.
He presents himself to the reader; he describes his daily life in
the Custom-House; he "discovers" the scarlet letter; finally, he is
liberated to write his novel. An examination of the functions
served by each of these phases of "The Custom-House" will make
it possible to propose a hypothesis not only for unifying the essay
itself, but also for integrating it into the overall fictional structure which Hawthorne produced.

At the beginning of "The Custom-House" Hawthorne invites
us, as surely as any Walt Whitman, to commune with his soul.
Hawthorne was a romantic, and he would like us to be among
"the few who will understand him, better than most of his school-

mates and lifemates" (3). But the strong defensive tone makes
the mention of Whitman seem incongruous. Hawthorne is de-
cidedly not like "some authors" who:

> indulge themselves in such confidential depths of revelation as
> could fittingly be addressed, only and exclusively, to the one
> heart and mind of perfect sympathy; as if the printed book,
> thrown at large on the wide world, were certain to find out
> the divided segment of the writer's own nature, and complete
> his circle of existence by bringing him into communion with
> it. (3-4)

Hawthorne is concerned to keep "the inmost Me behind its veil"
(4), and to do this he allows us the strictly defined role of
"friend, a kind and apprehensive, though not the closest friend"
(4). With this understanding of the relationship between writer
and reader clarified, Hawthorne proceeds through the Custom-
House setting and an explanation of his ancestral ties to Salem,
to present himself with clear dimensions in space and time.

Hawthorne wants us to meet him precisely in the setting of the
Custom-House and at that time of his career. His description of
the Custom-House is detailed, exact, vivid as the writing of his
American Notebooks had taught him to be. But he is not simply
giving "a faint representation of a mode of life not heretofore
described" (4). His thematic concerns are at work as well. He
evokes the dull atmosphere of the place and the lazy unrespon-
siveness of the people by contrasting them with a time when the
busy world of commerce had not yet passed Salem by. The
slovenly emptiness of his office is described with the same detail,
and it is here that he arranges for our introduction:

> And here, some six months ago,—pacing from corner to cor-
>
> ner, or lounging on the long-legged stool, with his elbow on
> the desk, and his eyes wandering up and down the columns of
> the morning newspaper,—you might have recognized, honored
> reader, the same individual who welcomed you into his cheery
> little study, where the sunshine glimmered so pleasantly through
> the willow branches, on the western side of the Old Manse. (8)

The obvious incongruity of the man and the setting, reinforced
by the allusion to the very different setting of the Old Manse,

must strike the reader as a suggestion in advance of the kind of incongruities which will be developed in *The Scarlet Letter*. As the world of the Custom-House was totally unwilling and unable to take account of the rich sensibilities of an artist like Hawthorne, so the world of the Puritans was unwilling and unable to take account of the rich femininity of a woman like Hester.[14] Hawthorne was stifled by this indifferent world, and it is not at all surprising that his experience of that world should project itself as a major theme of the story which evolves out of his Custom-House experience.

Perhaps there is an allusion to the same tension between the sensitive individual and the insensitive official world in the allegorical vignette which intrudes itself into the description of the Custom-House:

> Over the entrance hovers an enormous specimen of the American eagle, with outspread wings, a shield before her breast, and, if I recollect aright, a bunch of intermingled thunderbolts and barbed arrows in each claw. With the customary infirmity of temper that characterizes this unhappy fowl, she appears, by the fierceness of her beak and eye and the general truculency of her attitude to threaten mischief to the inoffensive community; and especially to warn all citizens, careful of their safety, against intruding on the premises which she overshadows with her wings. Nevertheless, vixenly as she looks, many people are seeking, at this very moment, to shelter themselves under the wing of the federal eagle; imagining, I presume, that her bosom has all the softness and snugness of an eiderdown pillow. But she has no great tenderness, even in her best of moods, and sooner or later,—oftener soon than late,— is apt to fling off her nestlings with a scratch of her claw, a dab of her beak, or a rankling wound from her barbed arrows. (5)[15]

Another thematic parallel between the essay and the novel is Hawthorne's discussion of his ancestral ties with Salem. There is a certain fatality, attributable to Hawthorne's ambivalent but strong feelings about his ancestors, which explains his return to Salem and his assumption of the post of surveyor. Those ancestors were a present reality to him. They bound him, at least for the moment, to the place, as Hester's ties to her Puritan world bound her to stay and live out her punishment. Hawthorne too is living out a kind of punishment—a punishment incurred by the severity of his first ancestor toward a woman not altogether unlike the heroine of Hawthorne's story:

> He was likewise a bitter persecutor; as witness the Quakers, who have remembered him in their histories, and relate an incident of his hard severity towards a woman of their sect, which will last longer, it is to be feared, than any record of his better deeds, although these were many. (9)

Hawthorne is able to pay off the debt incurred by this ancestor because he is so fully endowed with a sensibility which understands and shares the plight of a woman like Hester.

The care with which Hawthorne builds up the setting in which he introduces himself to his reader has a function, however, that goes beyond the mere suggestion of themes that will be important in the novel. This function is structural, an element of the fictional form. If we return once more to that carefully guarded distance established between the author and his reader, we may further reflect that the distance that Hawthorne has established is not simply a distance between author and reader, but a distance between reader and story as well. Here, I think, is the central purpose of Hawthorne's introduction of himself in "The Custom-House."

The aim, in a realistic novel, is to make the reader feel that the story world is not a story world at all, but a simple presentation of reality as it is. One aspect of this is that the creator hides himself from the reader. The absence of the authorial personality sets up an unspoken understanding between creator and reader that there is an identity between their points of view. By the artistry of the writer, the reader is induced to immerse himself in the story world, in its places and events, in its values, too, because the reader has been made to feel that the story world is simply his own world, and not the product of another human imagination.[16] Of course, the reader who comes to a realistic novel with his critical faculties fully alert may not allow himself to enter so fully into the world of the novel, but it is not impos-

sible that this kind of sophistication may in some cases be a
block to the specific kind of artistic experience which is particular to the realistic novel. More will be said about this later
in discussing Hawthorne's pivotal position in the evolution of
modern reading habits.

To place oneself, however, as Hawthorne does, clearly and
boldly before the reader is to create a different kind of relationship between the reader and the story than the one established
by the techniques of realism or by traditional narrative in general.[17] Because the author's presence is explicit, the story world
he presents exists precisely as *his* world, created, fabricated by
him. It is an "other world," not the reader's own world, and so
he neither immerses himself in it, nor discovers himself immersed
in it, but regards it from the outside, contemplatively. The story
is kept at a sufficient emotional distance for us to stand apart
and look for its meaning.

This difference in the mode of existence of a story world whose
creator is present relates to what we have observed about the
allegorical world of some of the sketches. Within the framework
of authorial presence created by the historical essay the actual
story evokes an almost surrealistic world, in which events proceed in ritual progression and are interconnected by an implicit
magical causality. We recognize this world as Hawthorne's world
of "romance," but we also see the effect as more than merely
atmospheric. Such non-mimetic objectivity demands intellectual
interpretation. Mimesis has been sacrificed to meaning by the
creation of a world where realism is not the artist's central concern. The author, by insisting upon his own presence, keeps us
outside the story world he creates, in order to keep our interpretative faculties alert for the more explicitly intellectual task
he has put before us.

The effect is maintained throughout "The Custom-House" by
the continued autobiographical tone, but it is also continued in
the novel proper. Hawthorne interjects into the narrative of *The
Scarlet Letter* a steady punctuation of brief historical essays addressed directly to the reader. They keep the story anchored in
its historical setting, and they keep the author clearly in view.

Primarily, then, Hawthorne's introduction of himself at the
beginning of "The Custom-House" orients the reader toward a

more detached and intellectualized fictional world. Secondarily, certain central themes of the novel find their parallels in the sensibilities of Hawthorne himself: the contrast between the sensitive individual and the obtuse world of ordinary men, the ambivalent emotional bonds of love, hate, and guilt which bind people to the place of their deepest suffering.

The second phase of the Custom-House essay consists of two somewhat extended character sketches set among Hawthorne's witty reflections on the people who populated the Custom-House and their influence on his ability to create literature. Here the theme of incongruity between the author and his associates becomes more important. Hawthorne maintains the proportion: Hawthorne is to the Custom-House world as Hester is to the Puritan world, but he takes it a step farther. Just as Hester is able to turn the tables on her punishers by making the scarlet letter signify angel rather than adulteress without herself repenting; so Hawthorne, by his seemingly harmless and irrelevant skill as a writer is able to make the impervious world of Custom-House veterans wince with pain. Hawthorne's smooth syntax proves to be the gleam on a destructive weapon which Hawthorne enjoyed and used freely. And he felt quite justified, in his own sardonic way:

> It is a pious consolation to me, that, through my interference, a sufficient space was allowed them for repentence of the evil and corrupt practices, into which, as a matter of course, every Custom-House officer must be supposed to fall. Neither the front nor the back entrance of the Custom-House opens on the road to Paradise. (13)

Hawthorne's most destructive blow is the character sketch of the "permanent Inspector." With a cheerfulness and good nature that never suggests invective, Hawthorne empties this man of all human qualities, leaving him a kind of harmless beast. His sketch is the more damaging because he follows it with the more extended and truly admiring sketch of the "old General." The two figures are at opposite ends of the scale of humanity.

One of the most interesting points of comparison between the two men, in the light of the themes of "The Custom-House," is

the different ways they live in relation with their past. Here is
the permanent inspector's past:

> There were flavors on his palate, that had lingered there not
> less than sixty or seventy years, and were still apparently as
> fresh as that of the mutton-chop which he had just devoured
> for his breakfast. I have heard him smack his lips over din-
> ners, every guest at which, except himself, had long been food
> for worms. It was marvelous to observe how the ghosts of
> bygone meals were continually rising up before him; not in
> anger or retribution, but as if grateful for his former apprecia-
> tion, and seeking to reduplicate an endless series of enjoy-
> ment, at once shadowy and sensual. A tenderloin of beef, a
> hind-quarter of veal, a spare-rib of pork, a particular chicken,
> or a remarkably praiseworthy turkey, which had perhaps
> adorned his board in the days of the elder Adams, would be
> remembered; while all the subsequent experience of our race,
> and all the events that brightened or darkened his individual
> career, had gone over him with as little permanent effect as
> the passing breeze. (19)

This is the scherzo movement. As for the old general:

> He seemed away from us, although we saw him but a few
> yards off; remote, though we passed close beside his chair;
> unattainable, though we might have stretched forth our hands
> and touched his own. It might be, that he lived a more real life
> within his thoughts, than amid the unappropriate environment
> of the Collector's office. The evolutions of the parade; the
> tumult of the battle; the flourish of old, heroic music, heard
> thirty years before;—such scenes and sounds, perhaps, were all
> alive before his intellectual sense . . . . He was as much out of
> place as an old sword—now rusty, but which had flashed once
> in the battle's front, and showed still a bright gleam along its
> blade—would have been, among the inkstands, paper-folders,
> and mahogany rulers, on the Deputy Collector's desk. (23)

Hawthorne creates two still-living links with the Puritan past, each
of whom manifests qualities of that past which are important in
the story of Hester Prynne. One represents the final reduction to
animality of Puritan materialism and insensitivity to human feeling. The other represents the dying fire of the nobility and

idealism which was the inspiring motive behind the whole Puritan enterprise. What Hawthorne sees around him, in this dull and moribund world of Custom-House veterans is the crumbled remains of a world which was once able to hold these qualities in tension so that moral issues, at least for some, were as deeply serious as they are for him.

Hawthorne is proud of the flexibility in his nature which allowed him to associate with the members of such a totally foreign milieu. It is a point of pride with him that the overwhelming dullness and decay of that world did not win out against him, but rather enlivened his sense of irony. Eventually he made the indifferent Custom-House world wince at the power of his pen. There is, then, a kind of ultimate irony which inspires Hawthorne to place the discovery of *The Scarlet Letter* within this backwater of decay and death. Hawthorne's consistent technique of anchoring his stories of the American past in the American present gains a certain piquancy here. Within a society of decaying human spirits amid its piles of useless bureaucratic scribbling, Hawthorne comes upon a symbol which will carry him back into the intense vitality of its past.

Hawthorne constructs the fictitious narration of his discovery of the letter to arouse suspense.[18] He moves from an idle curiosity appropriate to the oppressive dullness of the Custom-House to an almost obsessive contemplation of the letter and an imperious feeling of filial duty to tell the story. And as this transformation within Hawthorne himself is dramatized, he prods the curiosity of the reader by a kind of forward-backward movement from vagueness to clarity. The steps of discovery are rapid enough, but Hawthorne persistently diverts interest into details that delay the movement of the narration. We are first diverted by Mr. Pue, his commission, and what was left of him when his body was exhumed. What we first find is only a scrap of faded red cloth with a certain mysterious quality from its being the work of a lost art. When we finally perceive that it is the letter *A* we are again side-tracked by Hawthorne into thinking of it as a badge of honor. We are left with a final mystery-making puzzle— the burning sensation which Hawthorne felt in his breast when he placed the letter there.

What Hawthorne has elicited here is a clear demand for interpretation of the letter. And this demand for interpretation which he himself has placed in the reader is his way of alerting us to the fact that in reading *The Scarlet Letter* we are reading an allegory. We have seen in the short stories that one of the standard ways of breaking through the reader's spontaneous tendency to accept the realism of a narrative is to make from the outset a clear break with realism, such as Dante and Bunyan do by means of the dream technique. For Hawthorne, the dream technique is usually more subtly employed. It is less an initial clue to allegory than it is a pervasive quality of the whole work. Hawthorne prefers to confront the reader, as he does here, with a physical object that demands interpretation. As he tells the story of the discovery of the letter, he himself plays with its possible meanings and induces us to do so by the sense he gives of freedom to indulge in such a play of the mind. There is no predetermined meaning. We contemplate it with him. And this is Hawthorne's clearest and most explicit invitation to allegory.

Hawthorne does not present us, then, with an invitation to solve an allegorical puzzle to which he himself knows the solution because he constructed it. There is more than an intellectual puzzle here. There is, he suggests, a connection so deep and so intimate between himself and what the letter represents that the touch of the symbol creates a burning sensation, causes an involuntary shudder, involves him and us in a process which is deeply personal, for all its contemplative detachment. Hawthorne's own experience of the scarlet *A* in "The Custom-House" is an integral part of the allegorical structure which he creates, as he will remind us at the end of the novel when he tells us how oppressive has been his concern with it. Hawthorne's experience of the letter *is* the allegory which we read in reading *The Scarlet Letter*.

If this is the case, Hawthorne must make explicit the relationship between himself and the past from which the letter came. He does not simply set his story in the past, he establishes himself in his own present and then moves by explicit and precisely measured steps into the particular moment of the letter.[19] When we learn of surveyor Pue we are told that he died an exact eighty years ago. And we are given an even more vivid sense of his antiquity when we are presented with the picture of his exhumed skeleton and its well-preserved wig. We are made to feel the movement back, to experience the pastness. Then, by a second clearly distinct step we move from the times of Pue back to the figure of Hester herself through the medium of the oral testimony of the old people of the time of Pue. Oral testimony is here, as always, tinged with the quality of myth. Hawthorne achieves, by these measured steps into the past, more than just the desired aura of romance, the heightening of shadows and the clarity of outline which comes from a distant perspective in time. He emphasizes that the movement back in time is a part of the meaning of his story, a part of the structure of his fiction. Again, it is Hawthorne's own experience of the parallels and the contrasts between that distant time and his own present world which constitutes the allegory. This is to say again what has been said before, that Hawthorne is the hero of *The Scarlet Letter*. Leslie Fiedler gives an interesting insight into the risks a hero such as Hawthorne was running in his experience of the past:

> Symbols of authority, secular or ecclesiastic, in ruin—memorials to a decaying past—such crumbling edifices project the world of collapsed ego-ideals through which eighteenth-century man was groping his proud and terrified way. If he permitted himself a certain relish in the contemplation of those ruins, this was because they were safely cast down, and he could indulge in nostalgia without risk. If he was terrified of them, dreamed supernatural enemies lurking in their shadows, it was because he suspected that the past, even dead, *especially* dead could continue to work harm.[20]

Hawthorne's ruins were the Custom-House and his ghosts were the permanent Inspector and the old General, but the psychology is the same. Hawthorne is doing more successfully what the Gothic novelists did, building the courage to live among the ruins of the past.

The final phase of "The Custom-House" describes Hawthorne's futile efforts to create his story while still employed in the Custom-House and the creative release which came with the loss of his position. In the course of describing his difficulties he gives us a detailed account of the famed aura of romance which he tried to create in his fiction. His romantic world had to be a

neutral area between the real and the imaginary, suffused by a
cold light which spiritualizes (the moon), and a warm light
which gives humanity (the coal fire). This world must exist
ideally, like a mirror image, at one remove from reality. Though
he is tempted away from this, his preferred fictional world, by
the siren call of realism, he recognizes that it is not in him to be
able to penetrate to the deeper import of the every-day world.
It is his own interior war with the contemporary world which
causes Hawthorne's melancholy. It frightens him with the possibility that he will become another animal-like old man, his
mind able to focus no further than the next meal. What he sees
slipping from his grasp is precisely the faculty which distinguishes him from these old men—the power to live free of the
contemporary world, to live throughout the whole range of his
sensibility, to seek out his adventures among the world of un-
realities. Once he is liberated from the Custom-House and sets
out to write his story, happiness returns: "he was happier, while
straying through the gloom of these sunless fantasies, than at any
time since he had quitted the Old Manse" (43).

Allegorical Function

The mythological hero, setting forth from his commonday hut
or castle, is lured, carried away, or else voluntarily proceeds
to the threshold of adventure.[21]

Throughout this consideration of "The Custom-House" evidence has been accumulating that the underlying experience
which we are being invited to share is Hawthorne's own. His
experience of the letter is but the trigger for an experience which
he chooses to prolong by writing the novel. The mythological
hero has been replaced by the modern artist-hero who invites us
to suffer with him. *The Scarlet Letter* is Hawthorne's own adventure over the threshold of the past, the land where he continued
to meet with his most deeply significant personal adventures. We
meet him in the Custom-House, an oppressive milieu into which

his situation as a financially unsuccessful writer has brought him. Here in this backwater world, where the opacity of the commonplace is intensified by its irrelevance even to the surrounding contemporary world, the restless impulse of Hawthorne's spirit is stifled and unquiet. Ironically enough, in just this stifling milieu, Hawthorne places the discovery of the symbol which opens his mind to possibilities for a new adventure into the past, the long dead world of his Puritan ancestors.[22]

The transition from this description of the Custom-House world to the discovery of the letter is a kind of autobiographical summing up: from the rarefied world of Brook Farm, Emerson and Alcott to the dull world of the Custom-House is at least a move toward the concrete. But the irony is of Hawthorne's making. He chose to make this precise milieu of a dying culture the matrix from which the story emerged. It must have been this experience, then, which brought full realization that the values of his Puritan ancestors were not dead but alive and active. The heady atmosphere of Transcendentalism had failed to present him with such a challenge. Faced at last with the actuality of that old world he realized the need .to test out his own supreme value, the sanctity of the human heart, against the crude commitments of that still living and sterile world to contractual duty.

One idea more than another has agitated American novelists from Hawthorne's generation to our own, and . . . this idea is what Hawthorne defined as "the sanctity of a human heart." We should cling to Hawthorne's remarkable and precise wording of the formula, and not shrink the matter to a mere question of "identity" or some polemic for the rights of personality. Understood as Hawthorne and James understood it, wrapped in unmistakable religious connotations, the formula has had an almost explosive power of suggestion for the novel in America (and, from Whitman onward, for poetry too).[23]

But before he can set out upon his spiritual adventure, Hawthorne must be freed from the mind-shackling world of the Custom-House. The image Hawthorne uses of death and resurrection is appropriate here. It is not developed, except as a clever way of narrating Hawthorne's demise as a politician; but it is the image of a kind of baptism into the romantic story-

world of the past. It is Hawthorne's baptism which constitutes
the allegory of *The Scarlet Letter.*

This incorporation of "The Custom-House" into *The Scarlet
Letter* as part of an overall allegorical structure of which Hawthorne is the hero does not materially change anything within
the story itself; Hester Prynne remains the heroine of the story.
Hawthorne is the hero of the composite fictional structure. Hester
is the instrument, the magic sword, which Hawthorne has created
to confront, in dialectic conflict, the values of his fathers.

Hawthorne's particular re-shaping of the allegorical form is
not a sport, an isolated offshoot of literary history. Scholes and
Kellogg note that "In Western narrative . . . the heterodox or
personal symbol system has . . . tended to replace the orthodox."[24] Edwin Honig gives this remark its basis in the history of
Western thought:

> Some explanation for the elusive pattern and the increasing
> ambiguity in modern allegories may be found in the destruc-
> tion of the rigid base of cultural authority upon which alle-
> gory traditionally depended, and in the relatively greater stress
> put upon the autonomy of the artist since the Reformation.[25]

Hyatt Howe Waggoner makes explicit the connection between
these general facts of literary history and Hawthorne:

> But if his way of presenting the faith was more reasonable,
> less offensive to modern reason, than Bunyan's and Spenser's,
> it was also less rationalistic. Their faith may have been "false"
> in some of its elements, but it was a public, shared faith
> assumed to be objectively true, not needing to be validated,
> except in some ultimate and strictly personal sense, by the
> heart. . . . They could write more objectively because the dream
> that shaped their works did not seem like a dream at all.
> Their symbols could have the kind of objectivity that is pro-
> vided by known, public referents. They could be, in their own
> eyes and those of their contemporaries who shared their
> beliefs men of reason without committing treason to the
> heart.[26]

Certain critics do not seem to recognize that allegory evolved
as orthodoxy declined. Consequently they do not like to call

Hawthorne an allegorist. Robert Kimbrough, for instance, states that allegory

> does mix the Actual and the Imaginary; however, it demands a strict and well-defined philosophy or theology which it wishes to expound. But Hawthorne would join neither the "School of Philosophy" nor any Church; . . . .[27]

A. N. Kaul, speaking of Hawthorne, states that "the purpose of allegory is to strengthen, by an exercise of fancy, the received doctrine and the shared moral code."[28] Kaul's point is valid for the Puritans who people Hawthorne's story. But what is true of the Puritan allegory does not preclude the possibility of a larger allegorical structure which is itself a new and revolutionary rebirth of an old form.

The real argument for making *The Scarlet Letter* out to be an allegory is the analysis of the story which follows in the next chapter. But by provisionally granting the point for the moment, we can see what the nature and social ground of such an allegory would be. Because the medieval allegorist, and the Puritan later, shared a set of accepted values with his readership, author and audience could watch together as the allegorical hero proved once more the worth of those accepted values. By the time of the romantic era, however, the last vestige of this shared structure of values had dissipated. In this new world of questioned values, then, the author can not portray a hero whose victory, along with its moral meaning, is presupposed. Rather, armed with the particular values to which he personally, and perhaps alone, is committed, he places himself squarely before the reader and proceeds to share with him a test of the worth of his values by testing his own spirit in the creation of the story.

One might naturally object that if romantic allegory involves the presentation of the author's own particular set of values and not values which he shares with his readership, then the explicit presence of the author's personality should be a part of the structure of every allegory which comes after the breakdown of the world of shared values. Without trying to account for the structure of every romantic and post-romantic allegory, one may say that Hawthorne was particularly sensitive to the fact that most of his audience would not have recognized the breakdown of the common value system. They would still be subject to the presuppositions of traditional narration because they would still be likely to take for granted that there was a sharing of values between themselves and Hawthorne. Consequently, their discovery that in this story something more than the simple condemnation of adultery was at work would be bound to lead to a kind of scandal. Actual scandal did follow the publication of *The Scarlet Letter*. Typical is the often cited dramatic question: "Has the French era begun in our literature?"[29] Hawthorne has done his best to forestall this reaction. He does it precisely through his efforts in "The Custom-House" to distance the reader—to make him aware that the author's own depth of thought and feeling, and not a communal morality, is at work behind the veil of the fiction. Some early readers of *The Scarlet Letter* did not recognize that it was no longer possible to take for granted that every "good" story bears witness to a body of accepted values. Consequently they failed to recognize that in "The Custom-House" Hawthorne has presented himself as a man among men, separate and autonomous, free to present his own values for the acceptance or rejection of others. They failed to take account of the freedom which Hawthorne had left them and consequently they failed to allow Hawthorne the freedom which he was claiming.

Soon after Hawthorne's time, by the time of Henry James, at least, it seems that the American reader came to recognize the autonomy that existed as a part of the new relationship between author and reader. Only then could Hawthorne's specifically artistic qualities be examined in earnest. At first the reaction was extreme: Henry James claimed that Hawthorne was purely an artist, not really interested in values. Today we need not go so far.[30] We are able to accept artistic technique as integral with the expression of an artist's deeply personal commitment to his own values. Today we come to a literary work with a different kind of sophistication, trying to see it in itself, not as a reflection of our own social code. Consequently, the need today for the author to elaborate upon his relationship with the reader is less acute. Every sophisticated reader takes for granted the proper distance between author and reader, and manages properly to distance himself from the work he reads. Hawthorne, however, had to bring us through the transitional stage while Transcendentalism was making the final declaration that the hitherto impregnable tradition of moral values had broken down. He suffered acute ambivalence toward both the new and the traditional morality. He took care, therefore, to assure, by his authorial presence, established in "The Custom-House" and continued throughout the novel, an objectivity in the contemplation of his story that left him free to portray his ambivalence from behind the veil of his fiction.

NOTES

1 "Altogether inept," *American Prose Masters* (New York: Charles Scribner's Sons, 1909), p. 66.

2 "Curiously unsuitable," *Representative Selections* ("American Writers Series"; New York: American Book Co., 1934), p. xviii.

3 "Quite unnecessary," and "hopelessly out of harmony with the tone of the novel," *Nathaniel Hawthorne: Man and Writer* (New York: Oxford University Press, 1961), p. 56. Sam S. Baskett, in "The (Complete) Scarlet Letter," *CE* 22 (Feb., 1961), 321, gives a more complete list of the critics who reject "The Custom-House."

4 ("Phoenix Books"; Chicago: University of Chicago Press, 1953), pp. 9-10.

5 This is the central point to be made in the analysis of *The Scarlet Letter* which follows.

6 "Ambiguity in Hawthorne's *Scarlet Letter*," *Archivum für Neuere Sprachen* 198 (June, 1961), pp. 87-88.

7 References in parenthesis after passages from "The Custom-House" are to *The Scarlet Letter* (Ohio State University Press, 1962).

8 Henry James, Jr., *Hawthorne* ("English Men of Letters"; New York: Harper and Brothers, Publishers, 1879), p. 58. One of the finest books on Hawthorne, Edward Hutchins Davidson, *Hawthorne's Last Phase* ("Yale Studies in English" Vol. III; New Haven: Yale University Press, 1949) makes a distinction which must be based on James. On p. 143 Davidson says that Hawthorne was not personally interested in the operation of moral laws because his own life exhibited no violent concern with good and evil; but as an artist he was passionately concerned. I find the distinction unnecessary because I think that Hawthorne found in his art a way of expressing his passionate moral concerns, the only way for him. In this connection see note 13 below. Davidson goes on to say, p. 143: "Yet with Hawthorne we are seldom concerned with the eternal verities which men throughout all ages have agreed are true; instead, we often find ourselves facing moral laws which are mere conventions of an age." Davidson seems to have changed his opinion by the

time of his edition of *Doctor Grimshawe's Secret* (Cambridge: Harvard University Press, 1954), p. 8: "Behind every one of his preceding romances there had been some dominant theological idea which had been worked out and resolved according to a timeless morality." After instancing the four main novels, Davidson continues: "all these had been the resolution of some mature view of human society in its moral aspects." The distinction between concern as a man and concern as an artist seems to be irrelevant to this sort of thinking.

9 References in parenthesis after passages from "The Old Manse" are to Nathaniel Hawthorne, *Selected Tales and Sketches* (New York: Rinehart and Company, Inc., 1950).

10 Honig, *op. cit.,* p. 22.

11 "Hawthorne on the Romance: His Prefaces Related and Examined," *MP* 53 (August, 1955), 20.

12 *Op. cit.,* p. 101.

13 "These two writers [Hawthorne and Melville] represent, in fact, a third line of development from Puritanism, the only strain in which the rich paradoxes and tensions of Calvinism are not simplified in the interests of simpleminded orthodoxy or sentimental liberalism; and they engage in a common attempt to redeem the complex values of Puritanism from religion to art." Leslie Fiedler, *Love and Death in the American Novel,* revised edition ("A Delta Book"; New York: The Dell Publishing Company, 1966), p. 432. See also R. W. B. Lewis, note 12 above.

14 See John F. Lynen, *The Design of the Present: Essays on Time and Form in American Literature* (New Haven: Yale University Press, 1969), pp. 68 ff.

15 Edwin Fussell, *Frontier: American Literature and the American West* (Princeton, New Jersey: Princeton University Press, 1965), finds this allegory of the Eagle a significant bit of evidence for his own interpretation of *The Scarlet Letter* as an allegory of the frontier.

16 See the citation from Clara Reeve's *The Progress of Romance through Times, Countries, and Manners* (1785) in Robert Scholes and Robert Kellogg, *The Nature of Narrative* (New York: Oxford University Press, 1966), pp. 6-7. James K. Folsom, *Man's Accidents and God's Purposes: Multiplicity in Hawthorne's Fiction* (New Haven: College and University Press, 1963), p. 51, expresses this same distinction: "Romance achieves its effect by a kind of imposition of illusion *as illusion* on a reader, whereas a Novel achieves its effect by creating through illusion a sense of counterfeit reality."

17 Scholes and Kellogg, *op. cit.,* pp. 51-53.

18 On the historicity of the scarlet *A* see Gustavus Meyers, "Hawthorne and the Myths about Puritans," *The American Spectator* 2 (April, 1934), cited in Alexander Cowie, *The Rise of the American Novel* (New York: The American Book Company, 1948) p. 807, n. 88. For possible historical prototypes of Hester Prynne see Charles Boewe and Murray G. Murphey, "Hester Prynne in History," *AL* 32 (Jan., 1961), 202-204.

19 For Hoffman, *op. cit.,* this is the purpose of "The Custom-House," p. 169.

20 *Op. cit.,* p. 131.

21 Joseph Campbell, *The Hero with a Thousand Faces,* cited by Honig, *op. cit.,* p. 199, n. 11.

22 Professor Hugo McPherson, in his sketch of the overall shape of Hawthorne's fundamental myth, corroborates this interpretation of "The Custom-House," *Hawthorne as Myth-Maker* ("University of Toronto Department of English Studies and Texts," 16; University of Toronto Press, 1969), p. 15.

23 R. W. B. Lewis, "The Tactics of Sanctity: Hawthorne and James," *Hawthorne Centenary Essays,* edited by Roy Harvey Pearce (Ohio State University Press, 1964), p. 273.

24 *Op. cit.,* p. 98.

25 *Op. cit.,* p. 87.

26 "Art and Belief," *Hawthorne Centenary Essays, op. cit.,* p. 188.

27 " 'The Actual and the Imaginary': Hawthorne's Concept of Art in Theory and Practice," *Transactions of the Wisconsin Academy of Science, Arts, and Letters* 50 (1961), 284.

28 *The American Vision: Actual and Ideal Society in Nineteenth-Century Fiction* (New Haven: Yale University Press, 1963), p. 179. Hoffman, *op. cit.,* p. 173, seems to be on both sides of the issue. When he says that "fluidity of meaning is of course intolerable in allegory," he seems to deny that Hawthorne's own work is allegorical. But then he goes on to say that "Hawthorne's artistic method is to use allegory to destroy the absolute certitude of the allegorical mind." This seems to me to grant that Hawthorne is writing allegory. Hoffman fails to draw the formal conclusion that allegory has radically changed to meet the needs of a new age.

29 A. C. Coxe, *The Church Review* (Jan., 1851), cited in Bertha Faust, *Hawthorne's Contemporary Reputation* (Philadelphia: 1939), p. 506.

30 Some still make the distinction between personal concern and artistic concern, for example, Philip Rahv, "Hawthorne in Analysis," *The New York Review of Books* (Sept. 22, 1966), p. 21: "They [academic critics] have refused to see that Hawthorne's religiosity was of the surface only, not a matter of the deepest personal feeling but a traditional rhetoric he adopted as a protective screen for his fantasies." Most critics recognize that institutional religion meant little to Hawthorne, and theology less. But does that mean that morality means little, "is only a protective screen"? Rahv confuses religion and morality and signals the confusion in an earlier phrase, "religious-didactic." Suppose one grants that Hawthorne was deeply, pervasively neurotic. Does that mean he is a bad moral guide? Perhaps. Does it mean that morality is of no real concern to him? Absurd.

The Scarlet Letter

For the purpose of analyzing "The Custom-House" we have assumed that it is the introduction to an allegory. The test of that assumption is the present examination of the novel proper. The method of testing, however, is not *a priori;* it is not an attempt to show that a certain previously discovered allegorical interpretation works when it is applied to the story. Such approaches have tended to drift away from the texture of the story; distortions of emphasis creep in, and the reader has the vague awareness that his experience of the novel is being violated, that the analysis is unreal. Secondly, to accept a certain allegorical interpretation of *The Scarlet Letter* and defend it, presupposes a clear concept of allegory and how it works. But it seems much more valid in dealing with Hawthorne, in the light of what he was doing with the form, to let the concept of allegory form as the story develops. Consequently, the method here is to suppose that there are certain techniques which can be called allegorical techniques. That supposition has been examined in the first chapter. We proceed, then, on the principle that the presence of allegorical techniques indicates the presence of allegory. Held close to the story by the examination of its techniques, we have a better chance of arriving at that allegorical interpretation which the story itself suggests while at the same time perceiving the originality of Hawthorne's recreation of the allegorical form. The only strategy that seems appropriate to such an analysis by techniques is that of a running commentary, and that is more or less the strategy adopted here in presenting the evidence for the allegorical nature of *The Scarlet Letter.*

88

The Initial Ritual

The basic drive of Hawthorne's first chapter seems to be to elicit in his reader a pattern of responses which is appropriate to allegory. He approaches his story from the most universal of perspectives:

> The founders of a new colony, whatever Utopia of human virtue and happiness they might originally project, have invariably recognized it among their earliest practical necessities to allot a portion of the virgin soil as a cemetery, and another portion as the site of a prison. (47)[1]

All the conceptual elements of the Pauline interpretation of Genesis are contained in this opening reflection: "Wherefore, as by one man sin entered into the world, and death by sin; and so death passed upon all men for that all have sinned: . . ." (Rom 5:12). Utopia is Eden, the prison is sin, the cemetery is death.[2]

Given this broad conceptual perspective, when Hawthorne does get down to specific places, we are not surprised to find the prison door on Isaac Johnson's lot elevated into a universal symbol of sin: "Like all that pertains to crime, it seemed never to have known a youthful era." (47-48). To this symbolic door, Hawthorne opposes a rosebush which is also symbolic.[3] The visual and emotive contrast between the objects themselves might very well serve to elicit the reader's interest in interpretation, but Hawthorne makes certain of it. He assigns conceptual meanings as he presents his symbols. The door is "the black flower of civilized society" and the rosebush is the symbol that "the deep heart of nature could pity and be kind" to the sinner. This initial set of contrasting symbols is so emphatic that it becomes a visual and conceptual focal point for the reader's attention, and may very well remain so throughout the novel.[4] We may at least expect that the contrast between society and nature will be of central importance to the development of Hawthorne's thematic interests and so it proves to be.[5]

As we come to the beginning of the second chapter, we actually get a better insight into the function of the first chapter: to establish the allegorical mode. The first chapter has made no narrative progress. Chapter II begins at exactly the same place as had Chapter I. The opening sentences of the two chapters, juxtaposed, show interesting similarities and differences:

I	II
A throng of bearded men, in sad-colored garments and gray, steeple-crowned hats, intermixed with women, some wearing hoods, and others bareheaded, was assembled in front of a wooden edifice, the door of which was heavily timbered with oak, and studded with iron spikes. (47)	The grass-plot before the jail, in Prison Lane, on a certain summer morning, not less than two centuries ago, was occupied by a pretty large number of the inhabitants of Boston; all with their eyes intently fastened on the iron-clamped oaken door. (49)

In the first chapter, a throng is assembled before an edifice; here, "the inhabitants of Boston" occupy a "grass-plot before the jail, in Prison Lane." There, no mention is made of time; here, it is "a summer morning, not less than two centuries ago." There the people are merely "assembled"; here their eyes are "intently fastened" on the oaken door. The first sentence is without movement, time, or place. It is visual but not specific, and it is immediately followed by the universal reflection about sin and death which we have already noted. Adding to this Hawthorne's initial symbolic pair, the door and the rosebush with their conceptual meanings, we see how the first chapter has been constructed to elicit in the reader the reflective, meaning-centered response appropriate for allegory. The first chapter acts as the prelude to a meditation, it is a "composition of place."[6] It is vividly pictorial and yet completely static. It does not start the action; it starts a process of reflection and prepares us for many moments ahead when we will be forced to suspend our interest in the story, focus our attention on a symbol or symbolic tableau, and meditate.[7]

Hawthorne concludes his opening chapter with a self-consciously gallant offer of a rose from his bush. In doing so he draws attention to his presence as narrator. This explicit authorial presence is a part of his narrative purpose and continues the narrative stance he assumed in "The Custom-House." It works, as do the other techniques we have examined, to alert the reader to the allegorical genre. Consistently confronted with the author at the beginning of the story, the reader's tendency toward quick involvement in its concrete elements is frustrated. He is induced instead to reflect with the author on these elements as symbols which demand thought rather than as objects which make for verisimilitude. With this same purpose in view, Hawthorne reminds the reader of his allegorical intent. The rose "may serve, let us hope, to symbolize some sweet moral blossom, that may be found along the track, or relieve the darkening close of a tale of human frailty and sorrow" (48). Because *The Scarlet Letter* is an open-ended allegory whose meaning is not presupposed but to appear gradually, it is not necessary for Hawthorne to specify the moral here; but he is, as we have seen, especially concerned to establish the literary expectations appropriate to the genre of allegory.

The more specific opening sentence of the second chapter with its air of expectancy tends to project us psychologically forward into the story. But almost immediately we are brought to another full stop. Hawthorne, having established the reader clearly within the context of meaning-centered fiction and having given him a pair of visual symbols on which to anchor the thematic ideas as they arise, moves on now to establish the reader within the historical context in which his allegory is to be worked out. He does so by means of what is for him a kind of allegorical subform, the historical essay. It is, as we have seen, a favorite medium for him, one in which he continues to stand clearly before the reader, suggesting interpretations to him of the scene which is to follow.

Taking his point of departure from the grim rigidity of the faces in the crowd, Hawthorne reflects on the capacity of such a people to treat a sinner with sympathy. He asks whether they respect the principle which for him is at issue in the story, the principle of the sanctity of the human heart. The answer is a paradox. In contrast to society in any other place or at any later time, Puritan society cannot distinguish between offenses against society and offenses against God. Within such a world, the individual conscience, the "heart," has no distinct place. Yet, on the other hand, the Puritans are able, in a certain way, to give an awesome dignity to the heart. The awfulness with which every violation of law is punished argues a sense of the importance of human choices which in the later history of America will disappear.[8]

Hawthorne then narrows his focus to concentrate on the women in the crowd. He places them at a point along a line of evolution from the "man-like Elizabeth" through the coarse "wives and maidens of Old English birth and breeding" down six or seven generations to the delicate ladies of his own time.[9] He sees a connection between this coarseness and a certain public boldness. Progress in the refinement of woman implies, for Hawthorn, retirement from the public scene. Woman, as she advances through history, retires into a kind of citadel of privacy where we understand her to be the special repository of respect for the sanctity of the human heart. If this is the case, then what hope is there that we will find among these public ladies or in this crowd the reverence which is due to every human heart?

The drift of the dialogue which follows illustrates the paradox which Hawthorne has been considering. At first a group of ladies complains that the public punishment for which they are all waiting is too lenient. To them, the woman to be presented before them is a hardened sinner by the very fact that she is a sinner at all.[10] Most of all, they cannot see how any real suffering can flow from the mere wearing of the symbol. The crudeness of this complaint, however, is countered by a young wife whose more sensitive and personal intuition tells her of the interior suffering of Hester Prynne. Such an insight is not available to these women, and their grossness reasserts itself with new severity when the ugliest and most pitiless female demands that Hester die: "It there not law for it?" (51). The allusion here suggests the words of the Pharisees in St. John's story of the woman taken in adultery (Jn 8:5); and Pharisaism is the perfect characterization for the Puritanism we see here. But again there is a counter-statement, this time from a man in the crowd. He, like the young wife, insists on the importance of the interior: "Is there no virtue in woman, save what springs from a wholesome fear of the gallows?"(52).

This initial dialogue is arranged into a neatly dialectical pattern, a pattern characteristic of allegorical structure.[11] An iron

Puritan legalism is stated and restated; but to each statement is counterposed a contrasting and equally Puritan attitude, that of reverence and appreciation for the interior. We saw that contrasting attitude above when Hawthorne spoke of the peculiar awe with which the Puritans surrounded public punishment. Hawthorne's dialogue, then, is not realistic. It functions to illustrate rather than to dramatize. What it illustrates is the tension we have already begun to see within the heart of Puritanism. We may relate this tension to the contrast between the prison door and the rosebush. The Puritan people as a whole are more in sympathy with the iron social discipline symbolized by the prison door; but among them there are voices which, because of their respect for the interior of the heart, will be drawn to the mercy symbolized by the rosebush.[12]

It is only when this tension at the heart of Puritanism has been made clear that we are ready to encounter the heroine of the story.

> The door of the jail being flung open from within, there appeared, in the first place, like a black shadow emerging into the sunshine, the grim and grisly presence of the town-beadle, with a sword by his side and his staff of office in his hand. (52)

The image, "like a black shadow," which precedes the actual appearance of the beadle, and the official attributes which accompany him, are the clear signals of an allegorical personage. But Hawthorne is careful again to make explicit the fact that we are reading an allegory. "This personage prefigured and represented in his aspect the whole dismal severity of the Puritanic code of law . . ." (52). In conformity with his allegorical function and with the ritual nature of the action in which he is engaged, the beadle makes a solemn liturgical gesture:

> Stretching forth the official staff in his left hand, he laid his right upon the shoulder of a young woman, whom he thus drew forward; . . . . On the threshold of the prison-door, she repelled him, by an action marked with natural dignity and force of character, and stepped into the open air, as if by her own free-will. (52)

Hester appears in direct antithetical contrast to the beadle. Her action is a free act signifying her interior rejection of the role of sinner which is being forced upon her. She suppresses an impulse to hide the letter and looks around boldly at her neighbors.

The letter which she wears is as much a shock as is she. "It was so artistically done, and with so much fertility and gorgeous luxuriance of fancy, that it had all the effect of a last and fitting decoration to the apparel which she wore . . ." (53). The impact is totally at variance with the intended Puritan humiliation.

All that the beadle is, is his office. His individual personality is unimportant, hidden behind the gestures and attributes of his position in Puritan society. But Hester stands forth in defiance of that society. She has taken the symbol which was to make her another allegorical figure in the Puritan allegorical world and, by force of an almost violent art, has turned it into an expression of her own defiant individuality. Her entrance is the refusal to submit to the allegorical role of adulteress in which she is cast by Puritan society.

Hester's refusal of the allegorical role of sinner makes it clear that the story is being written from a vantage point outside the confines of the Puritan allegory.[13] Hawthorne obviously does not see Hester as the Puritans do. What he sees is her beauty and dignity. He even suggests a certain sanctity—her beauty makes a "halo" of her misfortunes. He underlines as well her interior suffering: "To a sensitive observer, there was something exquisitely painful" in her beauty (53). The point of view which Hawthorne seems to adopt is the point of view of the young wife and the man in the dialogue above. Hawthorne stands at that point in American intellectual history when what was once a small voice raised among the Puritans in favor of the individual conscience has become a dominant voice.[14] In his story Hester is a figure like the sainted Ann Hutchinson under whose footstep the rosebush had sprung to life. Hester rejects the crude legalistic Puritanism of the crowd. Somehow then, in some as yet unclear way, she represents Hawthorne's rejection of Puritanism. We will see, as the story develops, how far Hawthorne is willing to go in making Hester the representative of his own principles.

The Scarlet Letter is so clearly built around its three scaffold scenes that the scaffold ritual takes on the quality of a structural principle.

We have seen in the short stories how Hawthorne uses the dream technique to indicate to the reader that he is dealing with non-mimetic, meaning-centered fiction. In *The Scarlet Letter,* ritual takes over the central function of the literary dream. As we have seen above, literary dreams are structured, usually, according to the author's conceptual scheme. It is, perhaps, not too far-fetched to say that ritual is the structured dream of a whole society.[15] It is a social event in which the members of society step aside from their normal activities and appraise themselves and their values as a society. Everything tends to become symbolic. The people are more than a crowd. They represent, by the presence of their leaders in ritual dress, with their attributes of office, an ordered hierarchy, the very structure of their society. The ritual moment is set apart from time, from the flow of ordinary happenings. It takes place within an arena which is also set apart—an altar, a stage, a pulpit, a scaffold. The symbolic objects and people which focus the attention of the assembled society are made part of an action which expresses the attitude of society toward them. Its social rituals, then, give Hawthorne the opportunity to present the society with which he is concerned in its most intense manifestations.[16]

As the literary dream of an individual character is structured by the author to carry meaning, so the ritual of a society is structured to say something to and about that society. For example, here the beadle accompanies his solemn announcement of Hester's punishment by an official Puritan interpretation of it: "A blessing on the righteous Colony of the Massachusetts, where iniquity is dragged out into the sunshine!" (54). Hester's punishment, then, is an allegorical celebration of the Puritan way of life. In public punishment, the culprit is the representative of forces which are undermining society. The people assemble into a hierarchically structured group in order to accomplish a ritual destruction of the criminal force. This may be done by the destruction of the criminal or, less radically, by so torturing the criminal that, symbolically at least, the crime is considered removed both from his heart and the hearts of the gathered assembly.

It should, of course, be clear to most societies that actually rooting crime out of the heart, if it is possible at all, is a very long and complex process, involving much more of the positive commitment of society than can be represented by a public punishment. Consequently, there is an awareness that the ritual action is merely a symbolic purgation and only hopefully actual.

But Puritan society does not seem to be aware of the limits of public punishment. Hester is not to be executed, but neither is she to be imprisoned, kept physically apart from society. The Puritan leaders want more than the protection of society. They must be given credit for wanting to change Hester's heart. It is the how that horrifies. Hester is not merely to undergo the punishment of the scaffold; she will be set off permanently within the community by the wearing of the scarlet letter. She is to be made, in other words, to continue to live off the scaffold, the allegory that she is being forced to enact on it. A society whose public ritual is made to extend in this way beyond the ritual arena and the ritual moment into daily life, is a society so committed to allegory that it has become not a mode of expression but a mode of life. The correspondence between concrete events and eternal truths becomes a presupposition of life itself. Primitive societies used this sort of sympathetic magic to control their gods. The Puritans are primitives who turn rituals into magic by trying to control the heart. They are unable to distinguish between symbol and reality, between social conformity and interior *metanoia*.

And so we come again to the double allegorical vision which we have discovered in the book.[17] Hawthorne must present us both with the Puritan allegorical interpretation of this ritual event and with his own. After the beadle has given the Puritan interpretation of Hester's punishment, a procession forms. It is composed of "stern-browed men and unkindly-visaged women," on the one hand, and "eager and curious schoolboys unaware of what is taking place" on the other. There is just a hint here of the society-nature antithesis. The pillory is given a religious character by its proximity to the first church. It is not necessary, by now, for Hawthorne to say that the pillory is a symbol of the sanctity of Puritan life. Hawthorne presupposes that allegory and goes on to his own meaning:

The very ideal of ignominy was embodied and made manifest in this contrivance of wood and iron. There can be no outrage, methinks, against our common nature,—whatever be the delinquencies of the individual,—no outrage more flagrant than to forbid the culprit to hide his face for shame; as it was the essence of this punishment to do. (55)

We do not need to be told what Hester symbolizes to the Puritans. But Hawthorne reemphasizes the fact that he looks at her from another vantage point. He makes us see her for a moment through the eyes of a hypothetical Papist in the crowd. To such an observer she would seem an image of the Virgin Mary, though, Hawthorne is quick to tell us, she is the very opposite of Mary in her role as the betrayer of motherhood and the antithesis of salvation. Though Hawthorne is here stating his own reservations about Hester, he does not surrender to the Puritan view of her. It is a favorite technique of Hawthorne to force us to view Hester from alien viewpoints. He does so in two other places in the novel: When Hester presents herself at the door of the governor's house, the newly arrived servant thinks the letter represents some dignity. At the final scaffold scene the Indians think the same thing. This is Hawthorne's way of periodically calling our attention to an allegorical dimension beyond the Puritan allegory, even when that Puritan allegory is imposing itself most firmly.

We have seen up to now the use of several allegorical techniques: symbols with explicit meanings, historical essays of interpretation, illustrative dialogue with a dialectical structure, and social ritual action. We have seen something of allegorical characterization in the treatment of the crowd and the beadle. We have also seen Hester deliberately break out of this allegorical pattern. It is now time to move to a deeper level of Hester's character and to a deeper level of Hawthorne's allegorical characterization as well.

Ritual for a moment fades out as Hawthorne draws us into Hester's memory. From that vantage point we survey the whole course of her life, that which is individual and personal, antecedent to and free of her new allegorical role. What had been a vital human history, we see now drawn to a focus in the two realities which remain to her, the child and the letter. Her pain is the constriction of a personal life into the life of a symbol.

We are engaged here with a paradox. We see both the allegorical Hester created by the Puritans and Hawthorne's Hester,

more real, more mimetic, yet still a character in an allegory,
Hawthorne's larger allegory. She exists then, in tension between
two allegorical roles, one of which is quite close to mimetic
characterization. This, according to Robert Scholes and Robert
Kellogg, is characteristic of Hawthorne:

> It is highly likely that Hawthorne himself never settled con-
> sistently into a posture of either representation [realistic char-
> acterization] or illustration [allegorical characterization], and
> that the power and intellectual complexity of his fiction is
> derived from an intricate process of oscillation between these
> two ways of creating a simulacrum of the real world.[18]

But this is not a matter of accident for Hawthorne nor an attempt
to gain the advantage of both kinds of characterization by blurring
the lines between mimetic and allegorical personality. Francis
Russell Hart, in an English Institute paper, adds another insight
to that of Scholes and Kellogg: The movement of a character
from real to allegorical in a work of fiction is a meaningful event
within the fiction. Hawthorne makes it a crucial event within
his own allegory when a character is transformed or transforms
himself into an allegorical figure.[19] Allegorization is a definable
moment in the story. We see it taking place here. Hester is made
an allegorical figure within the Puritan allegorical view of the
world. She resists this allegorization with all the force of her
personality. In order to show this, Hawthorne gives us an insight
into the individual realities of her past life, a stroke of mimetic
characterization. But her very resistance to the Puritan allegory
will make her an allegorical figure within Hawthorne's allegory.
The scar of the Puritan punishment marks Hester for life; her
resistance twists her into a figure of resistance. This we will see
more clearly as the story progresses, but for the time being it
is important to recognize that the central fact for which we must
be alert in studying the characters of *The Scarlet Letter* is the
event in which each of them passes from personal and individual
reality to allegorical figure.

Our first meeting with Chillingworth serves perfectly to illustrate what we have been saying about the transformation of
characters from real to allegorical in Hawthorne:

At his arrival in the market-place, and some time before she saw him, the stranger had bent his eyes on Hester Prynne. It was carelessly, at first, like a man chiefly accustomed to look inward, and to whom external matters are of little value and import, unless they bear relation to something within his mind. Very soon, however, his look became keen and penetrative. A writhing horror twisted itself across his features, like a snake gliding swiftly over them, and making one little pause, with all its wreathed intervolutions in open sight. His face darkened with some powerful emotion, which, nevertheless, he so instantaneously controlled by an effort of his will, that, save at a single moment, its expression might have passed for calmness. After a brief space, the convulsion grew almost imperceptible, and finally subsided into the depths of his nature. When he found the eyes of Hester Prynne fastened on his own, and saw that she appeared to recognize him, he slowly and calmly raised his finger, made a gesture with it in the air, and laid it on his lips. (61)

What we see here is the crucial moment in the life of Chillingworth. Chillingworth is, as we first see him, simply a man, a man of a certain inwardness, but nevertheless a man. When he recognizes Hester, though, he is convulsed. By means of the snake simile, Hawthorne makes it clear that his interior reaction is toward evil. The exterior convulsion is gradually controlled. We recognize, nevertheless, that the calm which covers Chillingworth's features is the calm of a man who has made a fundamental decision. We do not yet know exactly what that decision is. Neither, for that matter, does Chillingworth in full. We will learn what it is as it works itself out. Still, we have witnessed the crucial event of his life during which, we are made to understand, a fundamental moral direction has been taken. The allegorical figure that Chillingworth is throughout the story is something that he *becomes* here.

Chillingworth's characterization is frequently the object of critical complaint. Perhaps the reading experience of the novel furnishes a valid emotional foundation for this complaint. Though explanation can do little against such a reaction, it is still possible to show that Chillingworth's characterization is not gratuitously monodimensional. In that first moment when he recognizes Hester, he chooses to be what he is for the rest of the book.[20]

Even in real life, an exaggeration of a single dimension of one's personality at the expense of the normal multivalence of human life, makes one monodimensional. As this single dimension of the personality becomes more dominant, one begins to see such a person as possessed by some powerful force, rather than as one who possesses himself in freedom.[21] In other words, there is still a tendency to imitate the ancients of both Old Testament and classical cultures and think of the mentally unbalanced person as possessed by some kind of *daimon* (see the discussion of demonic characterization on pages 49 and following). Freedom is lost to such a person, and with freedom gone the possibility of change is gone too. Growth is not the development of wisdom and maturity but the intensification of imbalance toward monomania. In this sense, then, such a character is demonic. The emphasis is not on *evil* except insofar as the most radical form of human evil is the loss of freedom. When such a person appears in fiction, he becomes almost unavoidably an allegorical figure.[22] Chillingworth's dedication to evil is not a static thing, but it is not growth either. It is a consistent and unbroken intensity which destroys his freedom. Chillingworth, consequently, is a very clear illustration of the allegorical technique of demonic characterization. We will see, as the story develops, that the idea of the demonic character can be applied to most of the people in Hawthorne's novel. But there is a twist. Hawthorne does not simply use allegorical characters from the beginning. He gives their allegorical quality a psychological foundation, an event in which a real person becomes an allegorical character.

With respect then to both Hester and Chillingworth, we have to remember that though both *are* allegorical, both *were*, within the novel, real. The allegorical role which the Puritan world imposes on Hester is the basis of a psychological change which makes her apt for the more authentic allegorical role in which Hawthorne casts her. The conflict engendered between the reality of her individual life and the crude moralism of the Puritan allegory, twists her to the point at which she becomes limited enough in dimensions to bear a symbolic meaning. The Puritans saw only "adulteress." By her resistance to that imposed Puritan meaning she necessarily rigidifies into another kind of personality distortion. But by making us see the psychological process, Hawthorne makes us see an allegorical character whose effect on us is more powerful than a more realistic one would have been. Our difficulty with Chillingworth is the opposite. We recognize his devotion to evil so clearly through the course of the story that we think of him too simply as an allegorical character. What we fail to notice is that an event happened to him within the story which gave him the motivation to turn himself into a demon. His demonization was the partly free act of an initially realistic character.

To theorize for a moment, though allegory is meaning-centered rather than realistic, it is always impure. Its very vitality as meaning-centered fiction depends on the proximity to reality of the allegorical characters whose story it narrates. What Hawthorne gives us, is more than just allegorical characters. He constructs an allegory about a world which crudely and naively tries to make men over into allegorical figures. The resulting distortions of their humanity make them the vehicles he needs for the expression of his own deeply psychological allegorical vision.

Hester's punishment continues at the measured pace of ritual solemnity. Her name is intoned. She is carefully positioned directly below the ceremonial balcony on which sits the magistracy. The Governor is given his symbolic importance by his ceremonial costume and guard of honor. Hawthorne describes him not in terms of personality but in terms of the correspondence between his physical aspect and the ideals of the community. The Reverend John Wilson, who conducts the trial of Hester, is as allegorical as the Governor. The fact that he is merely a type whose inner reality is unimportant is made perfectly clear:

> He looked like the darkly engraved portraits which we see prefixed to old volumes of sermons; and had no more right than one of those portraits would have, to step forth, as he now did, and meddle with the question of human guilt, passion, and anguish. (65)

The magistracy is simply a group of allegorical figures of that wedding of divinity and the social order which characterized Puritanism.[23]

Within this context and in a way very like Hester's introduction, Dimmesdale is introduced. First come the allegorical figures, then Dimmesdale's contrasting figure. The implication is
that within this rigid hierarchy of Puritan externalism there seems
to be another who resists its crude allegorization of the person.
Dimmesdale is described, in contrast to the Governor and John
Wilson, as a person of interior depth whose inner life pervades
his exterior. His speech to Hester is rich with concern for her
personal pain, a concern which we have noticed in the small
voices raised in sympathy for Hester among the Puritan crowd.
He seems much less concerned with Hester's responsibility to
Puritan society than he is with her soul's peace.

By all appearances, then, Dimmesdale should be a true soul-
mate for Hester in her resistance to the Puritan allegorization of
the human personality. He speaks and acts as the one human
person in all that crowd who represents a deeper grasp on
human realities than the rest of Puritan society can achieve. But
once one comes to know Dimmesdale's true relationship to Hester,
it is easy to reflect back on the ambiguity on his words to her
here. All his concern for Hester's interior peace of soul and
right to secrecy can be interpreted as the desperate effort of a
frightened man to preserve his own secret from revelation.
Rather than personal integrity, then, we get, in Dimmesdale,
another twisted person who will come more and more to represent allegorically the underside of Puritanism, the side which
hides sin, as the Governor and Mr. Wilson proclaim Puritanism's
sanctity.

We have been introduced, then, within the context of Puritan
allegorical ritual, to three very interesting characters, each of
whom is interesting because of his own particular relationship
to the Puritan allegory of life, a relationship which gives him a
meaning in the larger allegory that Hawthorne is constructing.[24]
Hester suffers the Puritan allegory, but so twists herself in reject-
ing it that she becomes an allegorical figure in Hawthorne's
allegory. Chillingworth so convulsively reacts to his personal
loss that he decides to act out for the Puritans their allegory of
righteousness while living out, in Hawthorne's allegory, a role
as the personification of evil. Dimmesdale lives outwardly the
Puritan allegory of sanctity, inwardly a life of self-torture. He

becomes Hawthorne's allegorical figure of the ambiguity at the heart of Puritanism.

The curtain of blind Puritan allegory drops again over the scene as Mr. Wilson preaches

> on sin, in all its branches, but with continual reference to the ignominious letter. So forcibly did he dwell upon this symbol, for the hour or more during which his periods were rolling over the people's heads, that it assumed new terrors in their imagination, and seemed to derive its scarlet hue from the flames of the infernal pit. (68-69)

The interview in the prison between Hester and Chillingworth serves basically to further the plot. It clarifies the past relationship between Hester and Chillingworth and tells us that Chillingworth's crucial choice had been a determination to search out Hester's lover. It also established the bond of secrecy which will free Chillingworth to pursue his revenge, but which will later appear as an important clue to the character of Hester.

The emotional and thematic importance of Hester's entrance into the bond of secrecy with Chillingworth is emphasized by her frightened question:

> "Why dost thou smile so at me?" inquired Hester, troubled at the expression of his eyes. "Art thou like the Black Man that haunts the forest round about us? Hast thou enticed me into a bond that will prove the ruin of my soul?"
> "Not thy soul," he answered, with another smile. "No, not thine!" (77)

This is the first appearance of a motif which Hawthorne exploits more or less frequently during the course of the novel. The hint of diabolic possession through a bond with Satan plays about all the characters of *The Scarlet Letter*.[25] This is a central motif of the Gothic novel.[26] Most importantly for our purposes, it is an explicit use of the idea of demonic possession for the creation of allegorical characters. It is true to the historical setting of the novel and gives, as well, a certain hell-fired intensity to Hawthorne's larger allegory.

Hester and Pearl

Hester has had her dramatic moment, the moment of her allegorization by Puritan society. We have seen that the basic fact of her personality is the conflict between her awareness of herself and the Puritan reduction of her to the role of adulteress. Hawthorne returns to Hester after the trial to present her to us again, this time in a fuller exposition. He assumes once more the posture of essayist to give us a more ordered and detailed elaboration of the basic facts of her life.

> Giving up her individuality, she would become the general symbol at which the preacher and moralist might point, and in which they might vivify and embody their images of woman's frailty and sinful passion. Thus the young and pure would be taught to look at her, with the scarlet letter flaming on her breast,—at her, the child of honorable parents,—at her, the mother of a babe, that would hereafter be a woman,—at her, who had once been innocent—as the figure, the body, the reality of sin. (79)

He clarifies, as well, the fact that her resistance to this allegorization is not the sign of an inner freedom, though it might first seem so. She must stay in Boston. She too is possessed, possessed by the need to be where she must resist. Here we begin to get a clearer view of Hester's *daimon*. Even though she constantly resists the allegory imposed upon her by the Puritan world, there is a fatality about her resistance which gives the foundation to her allegorical role in Hawthorne's allegory, though its meaning is not yet clear.[27]

But Hawthorne is close enough to the ancient allegorical tradition that he does not limit himself to the merely psychological effects of Hester's alienation. The external circumstances of her life are symbolic for the Puritans, but for us, too. Her home is not only an abandoned cottage on the outskirts of the settlement, but it is on sterile soil and it looks over an inlet of the sea toward the forest. Her needlework, the art by which she had first expressed her defiance of the Puritan allegorization of her personality, becomes a symbolic medium of communication with the settlement. Public ceremonies, funerals, all such symbolic displays come to require her decorative art.

But it is not recorded that, in a single instance, her skill was called in aid to embroider the white veil which was to cover the pure blushes of a bride. The exception indicated the ever relentless vigor with which society frowned upon her sin. (83)[28]

The point is, that if the Puritan allegory is relentless, Hawthorne's own allegorical treatment of Hester is just as relentless.

At this point it may seem that the imposition of the role of sinner on Hester achieves its end and elicits even an interior penance. She lives an austere life and gives all she can to charity. She even rejects as sin the joy she feels in her art. Still Hawthorne's deeper probing catches a false note.

This morbid meddling of conscience with an immaterial matter betokened, it is to be feared, no genuine and steadfast penitence, but something doubtful, something that might be deeply wrong, beneath. (84)

What is wrong?

But sometimes, once in many days, or perchance in many months, she felt an eye—a human eye—upon the ignominious brand, that seemed to give a momentary relief, as if half of her agony were shared. The next instant, back it all rushed again, with still a deeper throb of pain; for, in that brief interval, she had sinned anew. (86)

Her inner life, which Hawthorne goes on to describe, is anything but the life of a penitent. To Hawthorne's deeper vision it is a life obsessed with sin, which she sees everywhere with a diseased acuteness. She struggles against her obsession, but finds no freedom from the searing inner scar of the letter. Though she subverts the Puritan allegorization of her personality, she does not escape from that radical reduction of the dimensions of her person which define her meaning: the restless figure of a vague resistance to society.

Pearl, as Chillingworth, is frequently considered a gratuitously, if not irritatingly allegorical figure.[29] Again, as with Chillingworth, perhaps this is a legitimate feeling about her which cannot be quieted; but her allegorization, as his, is something we can see happening to her within the story. Hester is allegorized by resistance to the Puritans. Chillingworth is reduced to an allegorical demon by his own moral choice. Pearl is allegorized by Hester.

Hester commits against Pearl the same sin which is being committed daily against herself. When she looks at her own daughter, she is as subject to the Puritan disease of allegorizing as are the Puritans themselves. Though she meditates on the fact that Pearl is a gift of God, destined for immortality, and her own only link with humanity, her consciousness of guilt keeps her from seeing Pearl as anything other than its evil result:

> She knew that her deed had been evil; she could have no faith, therefore, that its result would be for good. Day after day, she looked fearfully into the child's expanding nature; ever dreading to detect some dark and wild peculiarity, that should correspond with the guiltiness to which she owed her being. (89-90)

Because of her mother's incessant, frightened scrutiny, Pearl is fated to become the living incarnation of her mother's own desperate and wild resistance to the world.

> Her mother, with a morbid purpose that may be better understood hereafter, had bought the richest tissues that could be procured, and allowed her imaginative faculty its full play in the arrangement and decoration of the dresses which the child wore, before the public eye. (90)

It does not take much juggling of the paradoxes of psychological suggestion to see that Pearl, costumed as she is for the part, and directed in her acting of it by the fascinated fears of her mother, cannot help but grow up into an allegory of the scarlet letter.[30] Consequently, though it may seem that Hawthorne has arbitrarily created Pearl to fill an allegorical role, the creation

is actually the work of Hester. It is Hester rather than Hawthorne who attributes Pearl's personality to her own state during
pregnancy:

> Hester could only account for the child's character—and even
> then, most vaguely and imperfectly—by recalling what she
> herself had been, during that momentous period while Pearl
> was imbibing her soul from the spiritual world, and her bodily
> frame from its material of earth. (91)

It is Hester, finally, who sees Pearl as demonic:

> It was a look so intelligent, yet inexplicable, so perverse,
> sometmes so malicious, but generally accompanied by a wild
> flow of spirits, that Hester could not help questioning, at such
> moments, whether Pearl was a human child. (92)

Of course, the Puritan world reinforces Hester's imposition of
an allegorical role on Pearl. "An imp of evil, emblem and product of sin, she had no right among christened infants" (93).
And, of course, Pearl understands:

> Nothing was more remarkable than the instinct, as it seemed,
> with which the child comprehended her loneliness; the des-
> tiny that had drawn an inviolable circle round about her; the
> whole peculiarity, in short, of her position in respect to other
> children. (93)

Nothing more could have been done by the external influences
which surrounded her to make Pearl into the demonic personality
of an allegorical story.

As a kind of ironic twist, Hawthorne shows us how Pearl,
brought up in the ways of the Puritan imagination, lives in the
creations of her own allegorical phantasy.

> The unlikeliest materials, a stick, a bunch of rags, a flower,
> were the puppets of Pearl's witchcraft, and, without undergoing
> any outward change, became spiritually adapted to whatever
> drama occupied the stage of her inner world. Her one baby-
> voice served a multitude of imaginary personages, old and

young, to talk withal. The pine-trees, aged, black, and solemn, and flinging groans and other melancholy utterances on the breeze, needed little transformation to figure as Puritan elders; the ugliest weeds of the garden were their children, whom Pearl smote down and uprooted, most unmercifully. (95)

Hawthorne's suggestions that Pearl and the letter are in preternatural sympathy reveal the hand of the allegorist whose causal principle is magic, but, as in "Lady Eleanore's Mantle," he is careful to give that magical sympathy a psychological base. The sensitivities of a child might easily be acute enough to connect the peculiarities of her life, the strange fears of her mother, the hostility of the people with the obtrusive symbol of which her mother and all Puritan society were so obsessively and obviously conscious.

The concluding dialogue of the chapter on Pearl is again illustrative, dramatizing for us what we have already been told. It centers around superstitious beliefs in the demonic origin of children, and it makes vivid the fact that a child such as Pearl could not help but be precisely the allegorical character she turns out to be. The effect of such conversations was inevitable. Consequently we have again an allegorical character whose allegorization is an event within the story and a part of the meaning of Hawthorne's larger allegory.

The fact that Pearl was the product of Hawthorne's immediate observation of his own infant Una is not the paradox it may seem to be: a real child furnishing the fictional material for an allegorical one. An allegorist such as Hawthorne must have put as much allegory into the real world as he put into his writing. Una herself undoubtedly appeared to be an almost preternatural mystery to him. It was simply a matter of heightening the impish and the preternatural while furnishing it with the psychological base of Hester's nurture which allowed him to make a real child over into a perfect allegorical figure.

The point to be stressed then about all of these main characters is that Hawthorne has not abstracted them and forced them into an allegory. They are created within a historical world whose pervasive allegorical interpretation simultaneously imposed and verified itself. That allegorical vision, blind and rigid though it was, had an effect both on those who submitted to it and those who rejected it. It crippled them all, stunted their reality. To a historical vision such as Hawthorne's they were bound to appear one-dimensional. As "The Maypole of Merry Mount" almost spontaneously wrought itself into an allegory, so here, the characters of the Puritan world have wrought themselves into an allegory. Taking the cue from Hawthorne himself one may object that he became an allegorist because he was unable to cope with the multiplex ramifications of more real personalities. It is more pertinent to say, it seems, that Hawthorne and the Puritan world found each other. Hawthorne, for whatever cultural or psychological reason, was an allegorist; he discovered his own proper world in the world of the Puritans. He was far, however, from submitting to the simple patterns of the Puritan allegorical vision. He saw allegorically, but he saw, as well, the damage that a naive allegory could do to the human person; and he used the allegorical mode to expose the distortion. He does not blur the distinction between allegorical and realistic characterization. He sees that allegorization is an actual phenomenon of human psychology, and that insight transforms his own allegory into a kind of superior realism.

Puritan Society

All the principle characters are gathered together for a new encounter with Puritan society in the scene at the Governor's Hall. As far as the characterization of Hester and Pearl is concerned, the scene is illustrative of what we already know about them. It functions to shift our interest from them to Chillingworth and Dimmesdale.

However, Hawthorne uses this new encounter between Hester and Puritan society to develop somewhat his image of that society. What seems to interest him most about it is its paradoxical use of ornament. The occasion of Hester's visit to the mansion is the delivery of a pair of fringed and embroidered gloves for the Governor's wearing on some great occasion of

state. The house is of stucco and broken glass giving it an
incongruous brilliancy fitted more, says Hawthorne, for an
Alladin's palace than for the mansion of a grave Puritan. The
furniture is elaborately carved. On the wall the Bellingham portraits show the same incongruity: their severity is offset by their
ornamental dress, armor, "stately ruffs and robes of peace."
Finally there is the suit of mail "so highly burnished as to glow
with white radiance, and scatter an illumination everywhere
about upon the floor" (105).[31]

The Puritan effort, on the surface at least, was to transplant
English society to the new land. "Governor Bellingham had
planned his new habitation after the residences of gentlemen of
fair estate in his native land" (104). But Hawthorne's emphasis
on the Puritan need for glittering ornament is an attempt to tell
us something more about Puritanism than merely its proximity
to Elizabethan England. Ornament, as we saw in the short stories,
serves to create or make visible a social hierarchy. For instance,
when the Governor's door is opened by a footman, Hawthorne
feels it important to say that though he is a "free-born English-
man" he is now a "seven-years' slave." The paradox suggests
that the Puritan need to create a structured society has displaced
traditional English respect for the human freedom for which
society exists. The point is made clearer when Hester sees herself
in the breastplate of the Governor's armor.

> She saw that, owing to the peculiar effect of this convex mir-
> ror, the scarlet letter was represented in exaggerated and
> gigantic proportions, so as to be greatly the most prominent
> feature of her appearance. In truth, she seemed absolutely
> hidden behind it. (106)

While he subtly suggests this exaggerated Puritan emphasis on
social hierarchy, Hawthorne simultaneously suggests to us that
there is already a force at work eating away at it. When he
speaks of the Governor's garden, he tells us that the attempt to
transplant English ornament to America is not succeeding.

> But the proprietor appeared already to have relinquished, as
> hopeless, the effort to perpetuate on this side of the Atlantic,
> in a hard soil and amid the close struggle for subsistence, the

native English taste for ornamental gardening. Cabbages grew
in plain sight; and a pumpkin vine, rooted at some distance,
had run across the intervening space, and deposited one of its
gigantic products directly beneath the hall-window; as if to
warn the Governor that this great lump of vegetable gold was
as rich an ornament as New England earth would offer him.
(106-107)

This recalls the way Hawthorne first described the Governor's
Hall:

This was a large wooden house, built in a fashion of which
there are specimens still extant in the streets of our elder
towns; now moss-grown, crumbling to decay, and melancholy
at heart with the many sorrowful or joyful occurrences, remem-
bered or forgotten that have happened, and passed away,
within their dusky chambers. (103)

Nature is taking her inevitable toll of Puritan dreams. Nature
has won out over the Governor's garden in the shape of the huge
golden pumpkin and over the whole Puritan world in the shape
of the human history of joys and sorrows which will turn the
Governor's Hall into the decaying relics known to the people of
Hawthorne's time.

The idea of the force of nature brings us back finally to the
way Hawthorne stated the issue of Hester's right to keep Pearl
in the first place: "The public, on the one side, and a
lonely woman, backed by the sympathies of nature, on the
other" (101). Hawthorne began his allegory with the symbolic
contrast between the black prison door of society and the rosebush of nature. We saw an approximate parallel of this visual
nature-society antithesis in the contrast within the Puritan crowd
between society—the crude, legalistic majority—and nature—the
two voices raised in witness to the interior reality of the heart.

In this new encounter with Puritan society, then, Hawthorne
quietly pursues the same nature-society opposition, making subtle
suggestions that Puritan society will eventually succumb to the
forces of nature. Consequently, although the Puritan world could
place the scarlet letter on the breast of Hester and so exaggerate
its importance as to obliterate her personality, Hester seems to

be taking on a role as the human embodiment of a natural force at work within the heart of Puritanism which will eventually assert itself beyond all power of resistance.

When the party with the Governor catches sight of Pearl, the Puritan allegorical imagination goes immediately to work. She is a child of the Lord of Misrule from the time of King James. John Wilson wonders if she is a naughty fairy from the old country's Papistical past. Hester is called a worthy type of the whore of Babylon.

The examination of Pearl which follows ends in a stand-off between the plodding dogmatism of these Puritan authorities and the elemental natural force of Hester's motherhood. Pearl intensifies the irreconcilability of the two. Dimmesdale, as at the trial, breaks through the inhuman blindness of official Puritanism and makes them accept the validity of Hester's claim. Rather, he makes them see that Pearl is for Hester the incarnation of the letter and hence the proper prolongation of the Puritan punishment. Dimmesdale, in other words, interprets Pearl to the Puritans in terms of their own cruel allegorization of Hester. He does so, however, without falsely interpreting. Hester may be the figure of resistance, but there is buried within that resistance, and her instinctive natural motherhood, a morbid submission which has actually made Pearl a morbid projection of her own sin. Dimmesdale, however, does not represent any clear commitment to the inner validity of Hester's motherhood. She has, after all, threatened him: "Look thou to it! I will not lose the child! Look to it!" (113). We do not know how much it has been due to this threat that he found the eloquence to defend Hester's rights.

This second of Hester's dramatic encounters with official Puritanism concludes as had the first, with a hint of the Faust motif. Mistress Hibbins invites her to meet the Black Man. Hester refuses triumphantly and confidently, but we cannot be sure how long she will. Mistress Hibbins herself has as much confidence in an eventual conquest of Hester as did the Black Man himself in his dealings with Goodman Brown. " 'We shall have thee there anon!' said the witch-lady, frowning, as she drew back her head" (117). The threat of diabolic possession is as real, if not more real, than it was at that first encounter between Hester and Chillingworth in prison. It continues to be an important part of the characterization of Hester so that we continue to wonder about her. We have seen Hawthorne's deeply sympathetic portrayal of her as a representative of motherhood. But Hawthorne has not omitted the deeply morbid elements of her motherhood. We are not allowed to make her good or evil. She is certainly not a romantic heroine. Hawthorne's allegory does not allow for such simple readings.

Chillingworth and Dimmesdale

Through Hester's eyes we learn that Chillingworth has become uglier and more mis-shapen. This alerts us to his close observation of Dimmesdale. After Pearl has expressed her affection for Dimmesdale with such uncharacteristic tenderness, Chillingworth meditates ·aloud on the possibility ·of learning the identity of Pearl's father by analyzing her. It is clear that he has at last found his prey.

We have only seen Chillingworth and Dimmesdale in the moments of Hester's drama. Now we come to Hawthorne's treatise-like elaboration of their characters and their relationship. In portraying them, Hawthorne stays close to their character types.[32] One of the things the physician-type suggests is a magical connection with the power of evil. Hawthorne underlines this suggestion of magic by toying with the popular explanations of his arrival: "dropping down, as it were, out of the sky," "starting up from the nether earth," "an aspect of mystery, easily heightened to the miraculous," "He was heard to speak of Sir Kenelm Digby, and other famous men,—whose scientific attainments were esteemed hardly less than supernatural" (121). All of these hints are summed up and climaxed by the Faust theme:

A rumor gained ground,—and, however absurd, was entertained by some very sensible people,—that Heaven had wrought an absolute miracle, by transporting an eminent Doctor of Physic, from a German university, bodily through the air, and setting him down at the door of Mr. Dimmesdale's study! (121)

Saner voices found Chillingworth's arrival an opportune act of the hand of providence. To all appearances, Chillingworth is an exemplary Christian; and his association with Dimmesdale is readily categorized in terms of one of the Puritan stereotypes of human relations: Chillingworth takes Dimmesdale as his "spiritual guide." But the ambiguity of the physician type itself and the suggestion of the Faust motif infuses the character with a proper suggestion of evil.

It is only a suggestion, however, an intrusion of Hawthorne's knowledge into the simple Puritan view of the physician. But just as there were two voices raised in witness to Hester's interior suffering in that first crowd scene, so there will be those who see more deeply into the relationship of Chillingworth and Dimmesdale. But first we must see Hawthorne's development of Dimmesdale as a character type.

Hawthorne has not yet allowed us to see Dimmesdale except through the eyes of the Puritan people. To them he is different from the other members of Puritan officialdom, but not different enough to upset their allegorical patterns. His defense of Hester on the scaffold and in the Governor's hall does not upset the Puritan sense of the sanctity of his life or of his relationship with Hester. Hawthorne continues to present Dimmesdale through Puritan eyes as he begins his more formal presentation of him. To his people, Dimmesdale lives out the stereotyped paradoxes of Christian sanctity, as Chillingworth lives out the stereotypes of the physician. The Puritan sense of being in at the beginning of a new dispensation in Christian history allows the people to cast Dimmesdale in the role of a Father of the Church. Other signs of sanctity follow. His austerities are the cause of his failing health; his seemingly imminent death is the result of the world's unworthiness to keep him, though he himself may explain it— with the typical humility of a saint—as his own unworthiness to do the work of the Lord. He resists the demands of his flock that he care for himself saying that his desire is for another world. Within the larger allegory, this Puritan allegorical view of Dimmesdale is carefully wrought irony, but Hawthorne's exposure of that irony is very gradual and subtle.

The placing of Dimmesdale and Chillingworth in close personal association, like the other relationships of the book, has one meaning to the Puritans, another to the reader. To the Puritans it is an association which flourishes because of the obvious mutual stimulation which results from their disparate professions of scientist and theologian. But Hawthorne warns us of an opposition on a much more dangerous personal level:

> A man burdened with a secret should especially avoid the intimacy of his physician. . . . At some inevitable moment will the soul of the sufferer be dissolved, and flow forth in a dark, but transparent stream, bringing all its mysteries into the daylight. (124)

Here is Hawthorne's typical narrative method at work. First he tells us in conceptual terms what is going on, then he dramatizes, with concrete facts, the intimacy between Chillingworth and Dimmesdale.

It is at this point that Hawthorne begins to suggest a gradual awakening among the Puritan people themselves. In spite of Chillingworth's apparent piety, an instinctive distrust of him has begun to emerge. There are some who see Chillingworth as the devil's agent and the fires of his laboratory as hell-fire. But their perception of Chillingworth's evil nature only binds them more securely to their own view of Dimmesdale as the typical example of the Christian saint:

> To sum up the matter, it grew to be a widely diffused opinion, that the Reverend Arthur Dimmesdale, like many other personages of especial sanctity, in all ages of the Christian world, was haunted either by Satan himself, or Satan's emissary, in the guise of old Roger Chillingworth. (128)

The people have not yet broken out of the confines of the religious characterology which limits their view of the human personality, and they never will. Still, they grope towards a fuller truth about Chillingworth just as they begin to see Hester, never fully as she is, but at least in deeper terms than they could use when they first beheld her on the scaffold.

We have seen the Puritan people more or less at one with

their Puritan officials in their interpretation of people and events. However, as the story progresses, they begin to manifest a kind of wisdom, which, though wrong, is more merciful and open than official thinking. Hawthorne begins to speak of a natural sympathy of mankind in the mass which, in spite of the pressures of official thought, begins to arrive at its own conclusions. We catch a glimpse of that here. The people will come to represent more and more the force of that nature which is taking its revenge on the rigidities of Puritan thought.

When we saw Chillingworth for the first time, on the fringes of the crowd at the scaffold, we saw him making a decision which would govern his actions for the rest of the story. Hawthorne now expands that moment in order to show us the gradual development of a demon. At the beginning, Chillingworth had had the severe and equal integrity of a judge.

> But, as he proceeded, a terrible fascination, a kind of fierce, though still calm, necessity seized the old man within its gripe, and never set him free again, until he had done all its bidding. (129)

This is the process of becoming possessed. Hawthorne now shows us the way this man-become-demon has taken on the subtlety of Satan in torturing his prey. It is interesting that the form of Chillingworth's torture of Dimmesdale is allegory:

> I found them growing on a grave, which bore no tombstone, nor other memorial of the dead man, save these ugly weeds that have taken upon themselves to keep him in remembrance. They grew out of his heart, and typify, it may be, some hideous secret that was buried with him, and which he had done better to confess during his lifetime. (131)

Chillingworth does not accept the Puritan allegorical world-view. But he employs it with cold cruelty against one who holds on to it desperately. It is Pearl who clearly recognizes what Chillingworth has become. "Come away, mother! Come away, or yonder old Black Man will catch you! He hath got hold of the minister already" (134). Finally, when Chillingworth has uncovered the breast of Dimmesdale, we see that his transformation is complete.

Had a man seen old Roger Chillingworth, at that moment of his ecstasy, he would have had no need to ask how Satan comports himself, when a precious human soul is lost to heaven, and won into his kingdom. (138)

The development of Chillingworth's character is here completed. This is the culminating moment of his transformation into a demon.

But Dimmesdale too is drawing on to a kind of climax. He does not perceive the danger of his relationship with Chillingworth, and so the relationship which most tortures him is his relationship to his people. In this there are analogies with the situation of Hester. The Puritan people consistently misinterpret him as they do her. His deepest battle is very much like hers: somehow to fight free of the allegorical vision which makes him a saint as it makes her a sinner. But the more he tries to throw off his role, the more hopelessly he becomes entangled in it:

"The godly youth!" said they among themselves. "The saint on earth! Alas, if he discern such sinfulness in his own white soul, what horrid spectacle would he behold in thine or mine!" (144)

Eventually Dimmesdale begins to lose his grip on reality. Hawthorne describes his breakdown in another essay-like treatment; but he illustrates it, sums it up, and makes it actual by means of an anti-ritual which is parallel with Hester's, yet in point for point contrast.[33]

Hawthorne speaks of Dimmesdale's midnight vigil as both ritual and dream.

Attiring himself with as much care as if it had been for public worship and precisely in the same manner, he stole softly down the staircase, undid the door, and isued forth. (146)
Walking in the shadow of a dream, as it were, and perhaps actually under the influence of a species of somnambulism, Mr. Dimmesdale reached the spot, where, now so long since, Hester Prynne had lived through her first hour of public ignominy. (147)

Hawthorne, with characteristic explicitness reminds us to place
this ritual beside Hester's and compare them.

Hester, as she stood on the scaffold, emerged from her
memories to recognize that the child and the letter were reality
for her. Dimmesdale's realities are the unreal: visions which haunt
his nights of penance. Hester's ignominy was real because it was
public; Dimmesdale's is secret, and therefore unreal. Hester
ascended the scaffold at noon; Dimmesdale, in the obscure midnight. Hester had borne her ignominy stoically and silently;
Dimmesdale:

> was overcome with a great horror of mind, as if the universe
> were gazing at a scarlet token on his naked breast, right over
> his heart. Without any effort of his will, or power to restrain
> himself, he shrieked aloud. . . . (148)

Nothing happens. The Puritan world sleeps. The ritual is
empty because it is secret, and a ritual must be social to be at
all. Instead, Dimmesdale's excited imagination begets a nightmare gathering of Puritans in disarray discovering him in the
morning light. When his twisted imaginings force him to laugh,
reality responds. Pearl laughs back; and then, standing beside
the minister on the scaffold, she tries to bring him to make his
ritual real: "Wilt thou stand here with mother and me, to-morrow
noontide?" (153). But Dimmesdale's professional role, emptied
of sincerity and truth by so many years of hypocritical role-play-
ing, makes his response automatic: " 'At the great judgment day!'
whispered the minister,—and, strangely enough, the sense that
he was a professional teacher of the truth impelled him to answer
the child so" (153). But to this stiff theology Pearl responds with
another laugh. Her allegorical significance begins to emerge here.
She is the reality of the scarlet letter and the adultery. She works on
Dimmesdale as she has worked on her mother, as a kind of reality
principle. That sense of contact with reality is what had filled
Dimmesdale with life when Pearl first took his hand on the
platform, but he is not yet ready for it.

At this point comes the nightmare climax of Dimmesdale's anti-
ritual. The light of a meteor etches all the surrounding objects
and each of the three participants on the scaffold with the "awful-

ness that is always imparted to familiar objects by an unaccustomed light" (154). But this emotion of awe is the result of an upheaval in the very meaning of things: "All were visible, but with a singularity of aspect that seemed to give another moral interpretation to the things of this world than they had ever borne before" (154). Finally, we learn what that meaning is:

> They stood in the noon of that strange and solemn splendor, as if it were the light that is to reveal all secrets, and the daybreak that shall unite all who belong to one another. (154)

The ritual, then, does have a meaning. We have moved back and forth through time, shifting our perspective from the confined and rigid allegory of the Puritans to the broader, more deeply human allegory of Hawthorne. He has taught us a certain historically conditioned moral relativism. But now Hawthorne's vision becomes eschatological. He affirms a moment beyond time and history when truth will be naked and absolute. At that moment what will appear is that one thing which is of value now, in spite of all allegories: the union of "all who belong to one another," the loyalty of person to person.

But Hawthorne indulges only for a moment in the contemplation of this eschatological instant of absolute truth. He seems to want to take it back. He makes us return once more to the Puritan world with its very narrow and limited interpretation of such phenomena, then to Dimmesdale with his own private interpretation: the projection of his own guilt into the sky in the form of a letter A. Still, Hawthorne says, there is a validity to the revelations of this meteoric illumination:

> If the meteor kindled up the sky, and disclosed the earth, with an awfulness that admonished Hester Prynne and the clergyman of the day of judgment, then might Roger Chillingworth have passed with them for the arch-fiend, standing there, with a smile and scowl, to claim his own. (156)

We are left uncertain, then, about Hawthorne's faith that there will ever be an eschatological moment of truth. We are not left uncertain, however, about the content of ultimate truth. It is the underlying and hidden reality of personal love and personal hate. This is the one truth worth grasping, the one truth Dimmesdale is not yet ready to affirm though he begins here to see it.

The final outcome of Dimmesdale's anti-ritual is a return to his futile repetition of half-hearted efforts at honesty, one more splendid sermon; and after the sermon, the whole Puritan allegorical game is elaborately played again. The minister's glove, found at the scaffold, must have been stolen by Satan. The moral: the minister must handle Satan without gloves hereafter.

When the relationship between Chillingworth and Dimmesdale has been brought to its climax, and we return to Hester. We find that her quiet refusal to submit to the Puritan allegory has gradually had an effect on the Puritans. She has made other meanings seem more appropriate to the letter. The way in which this has come about is important to Hawthorne's theme.

In the crowd on the day of Hester's humiliation a voice had been raised in opposition to the Pharisaism that surrounded Hester's punishment. This voice has gradually become stronger:

It is to the credit of human nature, that, except where its selfishness is brought into play, it loves more readily than it hates. Hatred, by a gradual and quiet process, will even be transformed to love, unless the change be impeded by a continually new irritation of the original feeling of hostility. (160)

While human nature may be ready to forgive, the officials of the society which had determined Hester's role were slower to bend:

The rulers, and the wise and learned men of the community, were longer in acknowledging the influence of Hester's good qualities than the people. The prejudices which they shared in common with the latter were fortified in themselves by an iron framework of reasoning, that made it a far tougher labor to expel them. (162)

What we see here is that nature, symbolized by the rosebush, heard in the voices of the young wife and the man in the crowd, and seen at work undermining Puritan rigidity in the chapter on the Governor's hall, has been at work among the people setting up a division between them and their rulers. The theme of nature against society is working itself out slowly and surely.

Is Hester, then, a kind of standard bearer or personification of benevolent nature? Before the prison door she was a figure of resistance connected, through Anne Hutchinson, with the symbolic rosebush. At the Governor's hall she had become a symbol of motherhood and elemental nature. But we began to see there how aspects of her personality betrayed a streak of the morbid. Here, the metaphor for her is that of a dead tree, a clear contrast to the natural richness of the rosebush:

All the light and graceful foliage of her character had been withered up by this red-hot brand, and had long ago fallen away, leaving a bare and harsh outline, which might have been repulsive, had she possessed friends or companions to be repelled by it. (163)

Hawthorne is not saying that life is gone from her but that it has been unnaturally repressed and springs forth in twisted shapes. Those shapes are thoughts. In a more natural life they would have been expressions of a woman's tenderness. If the Puritans had been able to know the actual effect of the letter, they would have been bound to feel that Hester had become more deeply perverse by her thoughts than even her adultery had made her. This would be the Puritan view; but Hawthorne, though he does not share it, does not deny it and then elevate Hester into the personification of the benevolent force of nature. Her freedom of speculation was no virtue nor source of peace to her:

Thus, Hester Prynne, whose heart had lost its regular and healthy throb, wandered without a clew in the dark labyrinth of mind; now turned aside by an insurmountable precipice; now starting back from a deep chasm. There was wild and ghastly scenery all around her, and a home and comfort nowhere. At times, a fearful doubt strove to possess her soul, whether it were not better to send Pearl at once to heaven, and go herself to such futurity as Eternal Justice should provide. (166)

Hester is infected with the essentially anti-feminine fault of intellectualism; and her intellectualism can lead only to self-defeat, because "a woman never overcomes these problems by any exercise of thought. They are not to be solved or only in one way. If her heart chance to come uppermost, they vanish" (166). This is not Puritan thinking, it is Hawthorne's own.[34] No character so far has become the bearer of Hawthorne's positive value.

However, though there was no real penitence or peace for Hester, and though she did not arrive at any clear conviction that would serve as an anchor to moor her, there is still a growth in her. Hester from the beginning had been sinned against. The first violation had been Chillingworth's when he married her. But she had repaid that violation by a sin of her own against Chillingworth. Both Hester and Chillingworth were victim and violator, guilty and injured. Hester, as a result, had to suffer a new violation of her heart, the crude Puritan punishment. But at the most intensely painful moment of that violation, she had tried to protect Dimmesdale by her silence. In her desire to protect him she had been led into a bond of secrecy which would result in a worse violation of Dimmesdale's heart than a revelation of his sin to the Puritans would have been. Hester has finally grown sensitive enough to perceive this.

> She had witnessed the intense misery beneath which the minister struggled, or, to speak more accurately, had ceased to struggle. She saw that he stood on the verge of lunacy, if he had not already stepped across it. . . . Hester could not but ask herself, whether there had not originally been a defect of truth, courage, and loyalty, on her own part, in allowing the minister to be thrown into a position where so much evil was to be foreboded, and nothing auspicious to be hoped. (166)

Her growth in sensitivity to Dimmesdale's suffering has given her a new courage in facing Chillingworth:

> Strengthened by years of hard and solemn trial, she felt herself no longer so inadequate to cope with Roger Chillingworth as on that night, abased by sin, and half maddened by the ignominy that was still new, when they had talked together in the prison-chamber. (167)

What we see in Hester, then, is a woman whose thoughts have led her astray but whose suffering has led her aright, to a new sensitivity, to a deepening of her respect for the human heart. She has not been able to grasp this new perfection intellectually in such a way as to achieve peace for herself, but she lives it.

Chillingworth, on the other hand, once he recognized that he had been victimized, chose to seek out the one who had injured him and to return the injury in kind. As his quest succeeded, his own objective became more clear, more purely vengeful:

> The intellect of Roger Chillingworth had now a sufficiently plain path before it. It was not, indeed, precisely that which he had laid out for himself to tread. Calm, gentle, passionless, as he appeared, there was yet, we fear, a quiet depth of malice, hitherto latent, but active now, in this unfortunate old man, which led him to imagine a more intimate revenge than any mortal had ever wreaked upon an enemy. To make himself the one trusted friend, to whom should be confided all the fear, the remorse, the agony, the ineffectual repentance, the backward rush of sinful thoughts, expelled in vain! All that guilty sorrow, hidden from the world, whose great heart would have pitied and forgiven, to be revealed to him, the Pitiless, to him the Unforgiving! All that dark treasure to be lavished on the very man to whom nothing else could so adequately pay the debt of vengeance! (139)

In terms of Hawthorne's ideal of respect for the human heart, Chillingworth has arrived at a point of total dialectical opposition to Hester. The revenge he conceives is not muddied by any gross human desire for the public humiliation of his victim. There is no alloy of any ordinary human revenge in him. He wishes the purest, most refined possible violation of Dimmesdale's heart.

The Puritans, had they known the facts, would have cast Chillingworth in the role of offended husband as surely as they cast Hester in the role of faithless wife. Hawthorne sees, however, that his own deeper moral principle is what is at work in the lives of these two people. According to that principle one becomes a devil while the other gropes toward a kind of human sanctity. We have, then, an almost complete moral reversal of two characters, which serves Hawthorne's allegory in clarifying the moral principle about which they pivot, respect for the human heart.

The present encounter between Hester and Chillingworth illustrates their moral reversal, first in terms of their relation to the letter. Hester insists that it is not a mere legal sign, but a deep interior scar.

> "It lies not in the pleasure of the magistrates to take off this badge," calmly replied Hester. "Were I worthy to be quit of it, it would fall away of its own nature, or be transformed into something that should speak in a different purport." (169)

Chillingworth is at opposite poles. To him the letter does not even have a legal meaning:

> "Nay, then, wear it, if it suits you better," rejoined he. "A woman must needs follow her own fancy, touching the adornment of her person. The letter is gayly embroidered, and shows right bravely on your bosom!" (169)

For Hester the law is not important; it is the scar on the heart. For Chillingworth there is neither law nor heart, but mere external ornament.

When they discuss Dimmesdale, they again illustrate the reversed position we have seen. Chillingworth can dare to ask, "What evil have I done the man?" before he finally lets "the lurid fire of his heart blaze out before her eyes" (171). For a moment he sees himself clearly:

> It was one, of those moments—which sometimes occur only at the interval of years—when a man's moral aspect is faithfully revealed to his mind's eye. Not improbably, he had never before viewed himself as he did now. (172)

But his reaction to this self-knowledge is to reaffirm his chosen dedication to evil: When Hester asks "Hast thou not tortured him enough?" his answer is, "No!—no!—He has but increased the debt!" (172).

For Hester, too, there is a certain moment of self-recognition, she sees the total futility of all her thought: "There is no good for him,—no good for me,—no good for thee! There is no good for little Pearl! There is no path to guide us out of this dismal maze!" (173). But she takes a word of this back. Though she sees a human devil before her, she still has the capacity to penetrate beyond the demon to the human core and wish good for him: "There might be good for thee, and thee alone, since thou has been deeply wronged, and hast it at thy will to pardon" (174). But Chillingworth has made himself incapable of such penetration. He refuses to see meaning at all. He renounces all responsibility, denying not only the Puritan allegory but the superior allegorical vision into which he entered at his first sight of Hester on the scaffold, and in which he has just seen himself as a fiend.

> "Ye that have wronged me are not sinful, save in a kind of typical illusion; neither am I fiend-like, who have snatched a fiend's office from his hands. It is our fate. Let the black flower blossom as it may!" (174)

Hester, at first a symbol of resistance, then the representative of the elemental force of nature, here appears to have won through as the representative of Hawthorne's fundamental moral principle: respect for the sanctity of the human heart. This is the hight point of her moral development, as it is the nadir of Chillingworth's.

What she has failed to become is what we shall see now. Pearl asks about the letter, this time with an altogether new seriousness. Hester denies it:

> "And as for the scarlet letter, I wear it for the sake of its gold thread."
> In all of the seven bygone years, Hester Prynne had never before been false to the symbol on her bosom. It may be that it was the talisman of a stern and severe, but yet a guardian spirit, who now forsook her; as recognizing that, in spite of his strict watch over her heart, some new evil had crept into it, or some old one had never been expelled. (181)

Hester says exactly what Chillingworth had said: The letter has no meaning. She has been bold and true with Chillingworth;

she cannot be with her own daughter. Hester's response to Pearl is a betrayal.[35]

Though Hester has become the symbol of Hawthorne's basic value, Hawthorne now goes beyond that principle. When Hester doubted her bond of secrecy with Chillingworth, she asked whether there had not been a defect of truth as well as a defect of courage and loyalty. Up until now the question of truth has centered on Dimmesdale; it has been more or less taken for granted in Hester because she alone, it appears, is living in the open. As the story moves now to its climax in the forest, the question of Hester's truth becomes as important as the question of Dimmesdale's truth.

However it is important to note, as the question of truth begins to move into the forefront of the play of moral questions, that truth here is a far deeper and more complex thing than *reason*. Hawthorne never goes back on the heart. He is not neo-classic, but romantic. As Hugo McPherson says, for Hawthorne:

> the realm of imagination is the realm of night, of moonlight and magic; it is in this realm that one truly "sees." Reason belongs in the daylight realm of empirical action, and is concerned with law, measurement, and mechanism. . . . In Hawthorne's personal vision . . . we have not a bipolar Head-Heart conflict but a tableau in which the Heart is central, flanked by two suitors—the empirical, daylight faculty of Reason and the nocturnal, magical power of imagination.[36]

The fact that Hester denies the letter to her daughter immediately before the forest encounter indicates how critics who interpret Hester as a moral paragon have failed to read the story. The allegory of Hester's moral elevation is over once her conversation with Chillingworth is over. Something else appears to be primary in Hawthorne's moral universe over and above the principle that Hester represents.

It is common among critics who read Hester as a moral ideal to be dissatisfied with the last pages of the novel.[37] But the forest scene, compelling as it is, is not so romantic as these critics would have it. Hawthorne never turns his story over to Hester, despite her emotional stature as a character of his creative imagination.[38] He has made her admirable, but has striven always to contain our admiration for her within limits.[43] These limits may or may not be dictated by Hawthorne's unconscious fears of her sexuality. On the conscious and literary level, however, Hawthorne's qualifications on Hester are not vague and unsatisfying. He defines her moral limits clearly; and he does so precisely in the forest scene.

The Forest

We have never seen Hester and Dimmesdale alone together. They have always met in the inhibiting presence of that official Puritan society which so oppresses them. The suspense built up within the novel by this prolonged evasion of a personal encounter between the lovers gives their meeting an emotional importance beyond that of any other encounter in the book. Hawthorne has an esthetic obligation to respond to this expectation with all the fictional power at his command. He must hold firm to his allegorical course while constructing a scene compelling enough and sufficiently real to win the complete emotional involvement of his reader.

The forest setting itself is the first object of Hawthorne's care in constructing the scene, and it is less the descriptive details than the meaning of the forest setting which he is careful to elaborate. He does so by means of a paradox. At first Hester appears to choose the forest for its freedom and openness.

> Partly that she dreaded the secret or undisguised interference of old Roger Chillingworth, and partly that her conscious heart imputed suspicion where none could have been felt, and partly that both the minister and she would need the whole wide world to breathe in, while they talked together;—for all these reasons Hester never thought of meeting him in any narrower privacy than beneath the open sky. (182)

But what she has actually chosen is a setting in which the sky is almost blotted out.

> The road, after the two wayfarers had crossed from the peninsula to the mainland, was no other than a footpath. It strag-

gled onward into the mystery of the primeval forest. This hemmed it in so narrowly, and stood so black and dense on either side, and disclosed such imperfect glimpses of the sky above, that, to Hester's mind, it imaged not amiss the moral wilderness in which she had so long been wandering. (183)

The open sky is elusive.

This flitting cheerfulness was always at the farther extremity of some long vista through the forest. The sportive sunlight, feebly sportive at best, in the predominant pensiveness of the day and scene—withdrew itself as they came nigh, and left the spots where it had danced the drearier, because they had hoped to find them bright. (183)

Pearl, nurtured as she has been in Puritan allegory, drives home the lesson:

"Mother," said little Pearl, "the sunshine does not love you. It runs away and hides itself, because it is afraid of something on your bosom. Now, see! There it is, playing, a good way off. Stand you here, and let me run and catch it. I am but a child. It will not flee from me; for I wear nothing on my bosom yet!" (183)

Pearl knows the allegorical meaning of the forest. It is the Black Man's world. Her obsession with the Black Man is a natural part of her own personality, yet it expresses Hawthorne's allegorical suggestions as well. She forces her mother to admit that the letter is the Black Man's mark. She knows that the minister with his hand on his breast is hiding another of his marks. Even the little brook which is otherwise so like Pearl insists that the forest is the setting of "sad acquaintance and events of somber hue."

But the little stream would not be comforted, and still kept telling its unintelligible secret of some very mournful mystery that had happened—or making a prophetic lamentation about something that was yet to happen—within the verge of the dismal forest. (187)[44]

Edward H. Davidson prevents a too facile criticism of Hawthorne's use of nature:

> He tended to set his human dramas against a vast, inscrutable, yet sympathetic backdrop of nature; sometimes this scenic design is in a point-to-point relationship with man; yet he did not fall into the most obvious fallacies: trees do not sigh, rain does not laugh, nor does the sky mourn. His tendency . . . was to frame the natural order as having anticipated and as having long ago enacted the drama of man; the human mood and emotion become, as it were, a duplication of what nature has itself long known.[39]

This, then, is the somber setting in which the lovers meet; and when they meet they are the images of dead souls. Dimmesdale is robbed of all vitality: "Death was too definite an object to be wished for, or avoided" (188). Hester calls to him faintly, hoarsely, and with a strange formality. She only gradually appears to him. At first

> he indistinctly beheld a form under the trees, clad in garments so sombre, and so little relieved from the gray twilight into which the clouded sky and the heavy foliage had darkened the noontide, that he knew not whether it were a woman or a shadow. (189)

Then "he made a step nigher, and discovered the scarlet letter" (189). Still, neither one of them seems real:

> "Is it thou? Art thou in life?"
> "Even so!" she answered. "In such life as has been mine these seven years past! And thou, Arthur Dimmesdale, dost thou yet live?"
> It was no wonder that they thus questioned one another's actual and bodily existence, and even doubted of their own. So strangely did they meet, in the dim wood, that it was like the first encounter, in the world beyond the grave, of two spirits who had been intimately connected in their former life, but now stood coldly shuddering, in mutual dread; as not yet familiar with their state, nor wonted to the companionship of disembodied beings. (189-190)

Hawthorne has recreated the world of Dante in the American forest.[40] The meeting in the forest is a meeting of souls in hell, souls frozen in the eternal state of a decisive earthly choice. The question that naturally bedevils the critic is why he has placed this all-important and climactic meeting between the lovers in such a setting. Did he create a hell in order to make the heaven that appears in a flood of sunshine only the more real? Or is he telling us that that flood of sunshine is illusory, a deception of the Black Man in whose kingdom it is merely a cruel way of redoubling the sorrow of hell? As Hawthorne develops the scene, I do not think he leaves the answer to this question ambiguous.

Working her way slowly toward the revelation that brought her to this forest meeting, Hester tries to make Dimmesdale see the goodness in his life. She exerts only a gentle pressure here, but it will become stronger soon enough. Hester is trying, against Dimmesdale's relieved admission of his own falsehood, to protect him from the reality of his life. She does not now, nor will she ever perceive the error in her deep desire to protect. She thinks she has come to the forest to rectify an untruth:

> "O Arthur," cried she, "forgive me! In all things else, I have striven to be true! Truth was the one virtue which I might have held fast, and did hold fast through all extremity; save when thy good,—thy life,—thy fame,—were put in question? Then I consented to a deception. But a lie is never good, even though death threaten on the other side." (193)

Despite all this, truth is still not her deepest commitment. She tries first to make Dimmesdale see good in the lie he is living. Soon she will overwhelm him with the prospect of living that lie elsewhere.

What Hawthorne is illustrating here is what he has told us so many times before. Hester is confused. Her loyalty to Dimmesdale is all-powerful. It would make her a moral paragon perhaps in a world where the supreme moral principle is respect for the sanctity of the human heart. But for Hawthorne, that principle is not enough.

For the moment neither Hester nor Dimmesdale has grasped fully the need for truth. What they see is the sin against the heart:

"We are not, Hester, the worst sinners in the world. There is one worse than even the polluted priest! That old man's revenge has been blacker than my sin. He has violated, in cold blood, the sanctity of a human heart. Thou and I, Hester, never did so!"

"Never, never!" whispered she. "What we did has a consecration of its own. We felt it so! We said so to each other! Hast thou forgotten?" (195)[41]

If we take this famous response of Hester as Hawthorne's, we take it out of context. Hester had sought the open sky, but what she actually chose is the dark forest, the image of her moral anomie. This is the Black Man's kingdom. Hawthorne reminds us of this immediately: "Life had never brought them a gloomier hour; it was the point whither their pathway had so long been tending, and darkening ever, as it stole along" (195). And even as he speaks of the charm that draws them to linger, he makes us see down the whole length of the road that they are travelling:

And yet it inclosed a charm that made them linger upon it, and claim another, and another, and, after all, another moment. The forest was obscure around them, and creaked with a blast that was passing through it. The boughs were tossing heavily above their heads; while one solemn old tree groaned dolefully to another, as if telling the sad story of the pair that sat beneath, or constrained to forebode evil to come. (195)

Dimmesdale's pathetic dependence on Hester—"Think for me, Hester! Thou art strong. Resolve for me! Be thou strong for me!" (196)—can be misleading. Hawthorne makes her so eloquent, so telling in her analysis of Dimmesdale's moral debility, that we cannot but believe Hawthorne must think her in the right. But to think so is to deny all that he has told us about Hester.

From the beginning Hester has followed an instinct telling her to stay here where the scarlet letter was placed on her. She has experienced the letter too deeply for it to be merely a legal mark. It has become the sign of her personality, and she will transform its meaning before she will abandon it. And when she returns to the settlement after long years of absence, she resumes it again. In a moment of weakness before Pearl she abandons her fidelity to the letter and to herself. The "good spirits," which would have to be her sense of herself, leave her and she becomes a prey to an escapist illusion. What's more, she insists that Dimmesdale believe in it too.

Her one great moral gift, her love and loyalty, her desire to shield the heart of Dimmesdale from injury, is at war with the truth. At the beginning she entered into a pact of secrecy with Chillingworth to protect Dimmesdale. She did protect him from the Puritan community, but the protection she gave Chillingworth exposed Dimmesdale to a far more malicious enemy. So here that same overpowering desire to protect Dimmesdale is at work. A conflict of basic moral principles, respect for the human heart and respect for a kind of total truth is unresolved in her. She is, Hawthorne has told us over and over, in a moral maze.

When Hawthorne describes Hester at the moment of her triumphant "Thou shalt not go alone!" (198), his orchestration of her triumph maintains an ominous rhythm of words that drum home the fact that she had been "estranged," had "wandered, without rule or guidance, in a moral wilderness," that she criticized without reverence, that her teachers had been "Shame, Despair, Solitude!" and that though they had made her strong, they had "taught her much amiss" (199-200).

Looking ahead for a moment it seems right to say that Hester has failed to learn that fidelity to another means not simply reverence for his sensibilities and pity for his pain, but reverence for the whole reality of his life, a reverence which restrains the desire to protect him from facing all the facts about himself. Dimmesdale's weakness, then, is no sign that Hawthorne affirms Hester's strength makes her right. Both are astray; one through weakness, the other through strength. Though the love they have for each other comes to a climax here, that love is no moral beacon to them or to anyone else. Hester is a woman whose protective love is destructive of truth, not of an abstract truth but of the deepest reality of her own heart and the heart of her lover.

It is important to realize, then, as we are swept along by Hester's rhetoric, that the whole meaning-drive of the scene and of the book has been constructed to deny what she is saying. It is not merely Dimmesdale's weakness which makes Hester's plan come to nothing in the end. It is the inexorable pressure of reality. Pearl, the only character in the book who achieves a kind of salvation, is, we shall see, the only one who insists that reality be respected.

The rush of joy, freedom, and renewed life experienced by Hester and Dimmesdale must be given its due. Dimmesdale is vitalized by his contact with the earth:

> "I seem to have flung myself—sick, sin-stained, and sorrow-blackened—down upon these forest-leaves, and to have risen up all made anew, and with new powers to glorify Him that hath been merciful! This is already the better life! Why did we not find it sooner?" (202)

We see also what Hawthorne meant earlier when, describing Hester as a tree stripped of its foliage by winter, he insisted that her sexuality was only hidden, not killed.

> Her sex, her youth, and the whole richness of her beauty, came back from what men call the irrevocable past, and clustered themselves, with her maiden hope, and happiness before unknown, within the magic circle of this hour. (202)

Hawthorne explains it all with his usual explicitness:

> Such was the sympathy of Nature—that wild, heathen Nature of the forest, never subjugated by human law, nor illumined by higher truth—with the bliss of these two spirits! Love, whether newly born, or aroused from a deathlike slumber, must always create a sunshine, filling the heart so full of radiance, that it overflows upon the outward world. Had the forest still kept its gloom, it would have been bright in Hester's eyes, and bright in Arthur Dimmesdale's! (203)

We have returned to the theme of nature which has run like a thread through the story. The rosebush at the prison door was called the symbol of nature's pity and kindness. Nature was the force at work in the great heart of the multitude allowing some to see deeper into Hester's pain and eventually to see a new, more benevolent meaning in the letter A. That same natural force of the heart was at work on those who saw the danger to

Dimmesdale in the strange companionship of Chillingworth. Nature in man is the "great heart of humanity" which forgives. Inanimate nature is the sub-human symbol of humanity's merciful heart. Nature exists throughout the book as the salvific counter-force at work eating away at the rigidities of Puritan Pharisaism. Hester and Dimmesdale are permitted for a moment to exult in the freedom given them by merciful nature. But it is only a momentary freedom from the rigid and inhibiting power of Puritan society. In other words, the society-nature conflict, important as it has been, has only a limited thematic value, just as respect for the human heart has only a limited value as a moral principle within the allegory. The superior force which transcends the rival forces of nature and society is difficult to name. Perhaps it is best called the force of reality. But what is clear is that the only adequate moral response to this force is truth.[42] That is the response which now begins to be forced upon Hester and Dimmesdale. Hester responds unwillingly, never fully; and as we shall see, she lives out her life in the gloom of her unwilling submission. Dimmesdale presents another question. For the moment, however, we may focus on Pearl.

The forest is Pearl's playmate, "it put on the kindest of its moods to welcome her" (204). She becomes a demon of the woods, "a nymph-child, or an infant dryad" so close is her identification with nature. But as she approaches Hester and Dimmesdale, her symbolic meaning expands again beyond nature to what it has been throughout the book.[43] The lovers see her

as the living hieroglyphic, in which was revealed the secret they so darkly sought to hide, all written in this symbol.—all plainly manifest,—had there been a prophet or magician skilled to read the character of flame! (207)

But they are led to misread her symbolism.

Be the foregone evil what it might, how could they doubt that their earthly lives and future destinies were conjoined, when they beheld at once the material union, and the spiritual idea, in whom they met, and were to dwell immortally together. (207)

Pearl will not accept their reading; she becomes a demon in her rage. But though to Hester's mind Pearl is a demon of the perverse, in the allegory of *The Scarlet Letter* she is a demon of truth. When Hester has resumed the letter, Pearl accepts her. She will not accept the minister however, and again for the same reason she had laughed at him on the scaffold at midnight: " 'Doth he love us?' said Pearl, looking up with acute intelligence into her mother's face. 'Will he go back with us, hand in hand, we three together, into the town?' " (212). Hester explains Pearl's reaction away with perfectly plausible psychological insight. But Hester, at the same time, senses that Pearl is right.

> With these words, she advanced to the margin of the brook, took up the scarlet letter, and fastened it again into her bosom. Hopefully, but a moment ago, as Hester had spoken of drowning it in the deep sea, there was a sense of inevitable doom upon her, as she thus received back this deadly symbol from the hand of fate. She had flung it into infinite space!—she had drawn an hour's free breath!—and here again was the scarlet misery, glittering on the old spot! .So it ever is, whether thus typified or no, that an evil deed invests itself with the character of doom. Hester next gathered up the heavy tresses of her hair, and confined them beneath her cap. As if there were a withering spell in the sad letter, her beauty, the warmth and richness of her womanhood, departed, like fading sunshine; and a gray shadow seemed to fall across her. (211)

Pearl is the symbol of the love of Hester and Dimmesdale, but of the whole truth about it, its sinfulness as well as its natural beauty. In the context of the meaning-drive of the allegory, Hester must resume the letter and Dimmesdale must publicly acknowledge his love. This is what Pearl's actions say. There is no evasion of the truth.

The tale is a sad one, Hawthorne tells us again as he told us before:

> The dell was to be left a solitude among its dark, old trees, which, with their multitudinous tongues, would whisper long of what had passed there, and no mortal be the wiser. And the melancholy brook would add this other tale to the mystery with

which its little heart was already overburdened, and whereof
it still kept up a murmuring babble, with not a whit more
cheerfulness of tone than for ages heretofore. (213)

The Concluding Ritual

Hester put on the letter at the end of the forest meeting and
became again the gloomy figure she has been throughout the
story. But Dimmesdale seems to be a new man.

If we think, with some, that Hester's plan of escape is the
dramatic realization of a new moral freedom, we must think
as well that the vitality which invades Dimmesdale is the benevolent effect of that freedom. The temptations he experiences on the
way back to the village are but the symptoms of the newness of
this sense. The inspired eloquence of the election-day sermon is
the triumphant result of this new freedom, and the scaffold repent-
ance is the contemptible relapse into weakness of a man who
cannot carry through on his convictions.

If, on the other hand, we think that Hester's plan is inadequate
within the context of Hawthorne's allegory, then we may go on
to say that somewhere between the forest and the scaffold, Dimmesdale underwent a radical conversion which gave him the
strength to confess. This often leads to the conclusion that Dimmesdale is the hero of the book since he is the only character
who undergoes a dramatic change. It seems to me that a close
following of `the text leads to none of these conclusions. More-
over, among those who make Dimmesdale the hero of the book
there is a kind of critical fallacy at work.

Although one experiences *The Scarlet Letter* as Hester's book,
critics seem to find it very difficult to remain true to this experience when they engage in analysis. Perhaps certain critical presuppositions intervene. One such presupposition might very well
be that *The Scarlet Letter* is to be analyzed as a drama in the
Aristotelian sense of an "imitation of an action." This supposition
requires answers to questions like: who is moving the action? and
who undergoes change? John C. Gerber and others who follow up

his article have centered interpretation on answers to the question of who is moving the action.[44] Henry James is the authority for going on to make Dimmesdale the hero of the book;[45] and though he has many followers, it would seem that both he and they have fallen into a kind of "mimetic fallacy." Ernest Sandeen admits that Hester is the "empathic" center of the book but goes on to say that Dimmesdale is the center of the "drama."[46] Since Hawthorne, however, has constructed his story in such a way as to elicit from the reader an interest in meanings and the evolution of meaning, analysis, should be less concerned with mimetic action, proper to the analysis of drama, and concentrate more on allegory, and the development of meaning. In this way Hester, because she represents one of Hawthorne's deepest moral convictions retains both "empathic" and thematic centrality. The fact that she fails to represent an even deeper moral conviction accounts for the shift away from her to Dimmesdale. Still, the shift is never such as to elevate Dimmesdale into the hero's role.

As Dimmesdale leaves the forest, he is filled with a disturbing sense of unreality. He looks back at Hester and Pearl in the forest to assure himself that what he has undergone was real and not a dream. Both the past and the present seem outside the grasp of his perception of reality.

> The edifice [his church] had so very strange, and yet so familiar, an aspect that Mr. Dimmesdale's mind vibrated between two ideas; either that he had seen it only in a dream hitherto, or that he was merely dreaming about it now. (217)

But Hawthorne keeps up the same ominous rhythm of disapproval of Dimmesdale as he had at the moment of Hester's "triumph." About his desire to conclude his career amid the panache of the election-day sermon, Hawthorne says:

> Sad, indeed, that an introspection so profound and acute as this poor minister's should be so miserably deceived? We have had, and may still have, worse things to tell of him; but none, we apprehend, so pitiably weak; no evidence, at once so slight and irrefragable, of a subtle disease, that had long since begun to eat into the real substance of his character. No man, for any considerable period, can wear one face to himself, and

another to the multitude, without finally getting bewildered as to which may be the true. (215-216)

There is no ambiguity here about the fact that the sermon itself is no sign of salvation.

Dimmesdale's perverse desire to do moral hurt to his parishioners is not a mere psycho-mimetic portrayal of symptoms. It is also a systematic sweep of Puritan society. The people Dimmesdale meets are arranged in a descending order of Puritan respectability: deacon, eldest female, youngest female, children, seamen, Mistress Hibbins. The coverage is intentionally complete. It says that Dimmesdale is driven toward the moral perversion of every member of his parish and even those outside his parish. The climax comes when Hawthorne touches once more on the theme of diabolic possession. Dimmesdale asks himself if he is given over to the fiend:

> Did I make a contract with him in the forest, and sign it with my blood? And does he now summon me to its fulfilment, by suggesting the performance of every wickedness which his most foul imagination can conceive? (220-221)

When Mistress Hibbins, however, puts the question with blunt self-assurance, the old, false Dimmesdale has not changed. He responds with the same ridiculous formality that he had used with Pearl on the scaffold at midnight, and he gets the same answer as Pearl had given, a laugh. The inability to face up to himself is still basic to Dimmesdale's moral attitude. This is what he shows in his desire to preach the election-day sermon. This is what Mistress Hibbins forces us to recognize. Dimmesdale has reached no moral heights. He is morally as weak as ever. He is merely a prey to the sinner's fleeting moment of exaltation.

> Tempted by a dream of happiness, he had yielded himself with deliberate choice, as he had never done before, to what he knew was deadly sin. And the infectious poison of that sin had been thus rapidly diffused throughout his moral system. It had stupefied all blessed impulses, and awakened into vivid life the whole brotherhood of bad ones. (222)[57]

When he meets Chillingworth, after his return, there is no new morality in evidence, only a game in which both are aware of the other's hostility and both skirt it with elaborate irony. This sort of ambiguous verbal brinkmanship we have seen Dimmesdale practice from the beginning of the book.

What there is in Dimmesdale, is a new kind of animal vitality that has lain dormant throughout the book, the animal vitality that must have been there when he sinned with Hester. It has since been repressed, but now it springs forth once more.[47] Dimmesdale delights in his march through the rough forest, he delights in his verbal sparring with Chillingworth, he eats ravenously, he produces the election-day sermon furiously, but morally he is not transformed. He is what he was, false, only more viciously so. Hawthorne gives no evidence of any other judgment upon him. As Hester is the representative of the moral inadequacy of the heart, Dimmesdale remains the representative of the falsity, the moral ambiguity, of Puritan righteousness. Neither hero nor heroine have so far achieved any moral heroism.

Hawthorne, at the end of his book, reconstitutes by means of a ritual the unchanged social texture of the Puritan world. The opening description of the New England holiday gives us the sense of a return to the surface of Puritan life. The forest scene brought all of our long involvement with its depths of personal pain to its climax. Now Hester is once more the muted public allegory of sin. Her gray clothing makes her personality recede so that the letter advances, revealing her "under the moral aspect of its own illumination" (226). But only a "preternaturally gifted observer" would have been able to detect in her any anticipatory glow of new freedom. Pearl is what she has always been, the incarnation of the letter and of that richness of personal response in Hester which has been obscured. Hawthorne creates the Puritan holiday scene through the dialogue of Hester and Pearl, then interposes another of his historical essays on the paradoxical Puritan love of ritual festivity. In the midst of this bustle of color and high feeling Hawthorne stages an almost operatic entrance of the sea captain with Chillingworth. One can hear the chords of the orchestra and feel the strokes of doom on Hester's heart. But Hawthorne wastes little time building suspense. He had never really allowed us to believe in the escape. The problem of *The*

Scarlet Letter cannot be solved by plot. Hawthorne hastens on to
the moral resolution of his story. And so we end where we began,
on the scaffold, where the problem of society and the individual
human heart was first proposed. This time we are armed with a
deeper and broader moral insight into the conflict.

The crowd takes its ritual form as the procession begins, a
more solemn and magnificent procession than the one which took
Hester to the scaffold. But Hawthorne makes us see, nevertheless, that it is the same Puritan world. Of this scene Marius
Bewley says:

> This crisis is enacted against a solidly realized background
> of civil and military order, and at this crucial moment of the
> novel the background has the effect of powerfully personi-
> fying that society from which Hester's and Dimmesdale's sin
> has alienated them. It clearly represents much more than
> was suggested by the rude inquisitiveness of the boors who
> gathered around Hester in the market-place. Without the
> resonance provided by this richly communicated sense of a
> more-than-Puritan society which we are given in such passages,
> the whole tragedy would lose stature.[48]

The authority-structure is based, not on the old value of nobility,
nor on the modern estimation of individual achievement, but on
"the massive materials which produce stability and dignity of
character" (237). The climactic order of the procession, music,
soldiery, the civil government, is crowned by the appearance of
Dimmesdale. The retiring, sensitive saint has given way to a new
person of ambiguous vitality who seems more fitted for the high
position which the ministry held among these people. Dimmesdale is every inch the role he plays. But it is experienced as a
role by Hester, who sees him as out of her reach, not the man
with whom she had shared such an intimacy as the intimacy of
the forest. Is it a man playing a role that we see? All that we
have seen of Dimmesdale up to that forest meeting would lead
us to think so. But we are meant to be uncertain. The whole of
the story now focuses on this man. Hester has had her moment
and been defeated. The malignancy of evil in the person of
Chillingworth has thwarted all hope of escape. For her all is over.
We have still to learn about Dimmesdale.

Hester takes up her position near the scaffold for this decisive ritual. Through her ears we hear the sermon as music. The words of the sermon are undoubtedly the words of the Puritan allegory, but that allegory is of little interest to her. She has rejected it from the beginning. All that is important to her is the person of her lover.

> The sermon had throughout a meaning for her, entirely apart from its indistinguishable words. These perhaps, if more distinctly heard, might have been only a grosser medium, and have clogged the spiritual sense. (243)

She hears the rise and fall of his voice as the anguish of suffering humanity.[49]

Meanwhile, Hester becomes the center of vulgar attention. Once more Hawthorne ventures that some, in this case the Indians, may consider the letter the sign of a high dignity. That had been his own first reaction in the Custom-House. He has used it repeatedly to keep our view of Hester distinct from the Puritan view. Hester sees the same group of matrons who had been at her first exposure on the pillory.

> At the final hour, when she was so soon to fling aside the burning letter, it had strangely become the centre of more remark and excitement, and was thus made to sear her breast more painfully, than at any time since the first day she put it on. (246)

Hawthorne binds up beginning and end, impressing us with the irrevocable quality of Hester's punishment in spite of any changes in the attitude among the Puritan people.

Hawthorne has built up his picture of the Puritan holiday through the eyes of Hester and Pearl, and we have heard Dimmesdale's sermon through Hester's ears. Now the narrative point of view shifts with finality away from the interior world of Hester and back onto the social surface of the Puritan world. The Puritans, of course, are interested in Dimmesdale's words because they are the words of the Puritan allegory. But Hawthorne's irony, though subtle, is unmistakable as he gives us those words. Whatever high and glorious destiny New England may have, it is not, from his standpoint in time, as a people of the Lord. Hawthorne does not say it is not, but the fact that he puts it into the mouth of Dimmesdale, who is at one and the same time the most admired of Puritan divines, and the most deeply sinful of the Puritan people, implies something about the validity of the message.[50]   The secret of Dimmesdale's appeal as a preacher, all these years, has been the secret canker of guilt eating away at him; and this sermon, we know, is the product of a climactic surrender to evil which released a vitality in Dimmesdale that had long been repressed. Dimmesdale's triumph is ambiguous, as Puritanism's must be. It is defeated by the undertow of personal guilt, as the rigid Puritan world is bound to be defeated by the imperious undertow of natural humanity.

After his triumphant sermon, the procession forms again amidst a massive shout of the people. But their shout is silenced by the appearance of the minister, feeble and pale. Predictably they misinterpret.

> This earthly faintness was, in their view, only another phase of the minister's celestial strength; nor would it have seemed a miracle too high to be wrought for one so holy, had he ascended before their eyes, waxing dimmer and brighter, and fading at last into the light of heaven! (252)

As Dimmesdale ascends the scaffold, Chillingworth is defeated. But the Puritan hierarchy, too, is defeated. Its world of clear meanings is upset and at a loss.

> The men of rank and dignity, who stood more immediately around the clergyman, were so taken by surprise, and so perplexed as to the purport of what they saw,—unable to receive the explanation which most readily presented itself, or to imagine any other,—that they remained silent and inactive spectators of the judgment which Providence seemed about to work. (253)
> Still, even this triumph is a profoundly ambiguous one.
> "For thee and Pearl, be it as God shall order," said the minister; "and God is merciful! Let me now do the will which he hath made plain before my sight. For, Hester, I am a dying man. So let me make haste to take my shame upon me." (254)

Is this the self-centered individualism so characteristic not only of Puritan material culture, but especially of Puritan spirituality? Or is it the psychological freedom of a man who realizes that the deepest and fullest love cannot intrude between God and another soul, that love has to recognize this limit inherent in the solitude of every human person? Does Dimmesdale, at the very moment when he has the courage to acknowledge his love for Hester and Pearl, renounce them out of fear for his own salvation, or stand free of them with the clear-sighted love of a man who knows the limits of love? It seems an unresolved question which leaves the meaning of Dimmesdale's character ambiguous with precisely the ambiguity that is at the heart of Puritan faith.

Dimmesdale turns:

> to the people, whose great heart was thoroughly appalled, yet overflowing with tearful sympathy, as knowing that some deep life-matter—which, if full of sin, was full of anguish, and repentance likewise—was now to be laid open to them. (254)

The confession of Dimmesdale is a confession about the scarlet letter. It is a revelation of its depths, depths which the Puritan people had failed to penetrate. But Hawthorne insists that these people are different from the crude multitude which had first stared at Hester. They are different as well from their rigid Puritan leaders. They are a people in whom nature has won out over dogma. Hawthorne speaks of their great heart overflowing with tearful sympathy. Dimmesdale calls on this natural human sympathy as he takes them with him beneath the legal symbol into the heart where the letter really exists and where they had not been able to perceive it before. The form of the confession is a step by step penetration of the interior reality of the symbol.

> He tells you, that, with all its mysterious horror, it is but the shadow of what he bears on his own breast, and that even this, his own red stigma, is no more than the type of what has seared his inmost heart. (255)

In such a climax which finally interprets a symbol that has focused the attention of the reader throughout the book, the characters themselves too must change. This is both a demand of psychological realism and a demand of the allegorical form. We have here another moment within the fiction when what it is that makes a character demonic or real is at work.

We saw Chillingworth change from man to demon at the beginning of the book, a multivalent human life gradually became demonic as his obsession reduced Chillingworth's existence to a single dimension. He became an embodiment of revenge, distilled to its most subtle and intense essence. But the object of revenge is now gone and his existence no longer has any principle of reality. Chillingworth disappears.

Pearl, on the other hand, has not had her chance at real humanity. The psychological distortion which has been twisted into her personality by her mother's guilt and isolation, and reinforced by the Puritan community, has inhibited the free development of love and the capacity to suffer. Here she is freed.

> Pearl kissed his lips. A spell was broken. The great scene of grief, in which the wild infant bore a part, had developed all her sympathies; and as her tears fell upon her father's cheek, they were the pledge that she would grow up amid human joy and sorrow, nor for ever do battle with the world, but be a woman in it. Towards her mother, too, Pearl's errand as as messenger of anguish was all fulfilled. (256)

Her father's confession has released her from the inhibiting allegorical role she has been forced to assume. She is the one character of the book who changes from allegorical to real. This transformation has been called the operation of a mere *deus ex machina*.[51] But if there is a lapse in characterization here, it is but a partial one. The relationship with Hester has been profoundly real.

Dimmesdale remains the ambiguous representative of the Puritan world. The vitality which came to him in the forest was not, in terms of the book, a vitality rooted in freedom, Christian or pagan. Perhaps there is no mimetic, that is, psychological explanation for Dimmesdale's confession. It remains tainted with ambiguity.

> The law we broke!—the sin here so awfully revealed; let these alone be in thy thoughts! I fear! I fear! It may be, that, when we forgot our God,—when we violated our reverence

each for the other's soul,—it was thenceforth vain to hope that we could meet hereafter, in an everlasting and pure reunion. God knows; and He is merciful! He hath proved his mercy, and most of all, in my afflictions. (256)

Perhaps the same fear which vitiated Dimmesdale's stance toward his people inspirits him as he stands before God. Dimmesdale remains, as he dies, the symbol of an ambiguity within the heart of Puritanism.

Only Hester is by-passed by this climactic event. Only her love for Dimmesdale is important to her. The revelation of the scarlet letter as well as its larger moral implications leave her untouched. For her, there has been much passion, but no fulness of perception. She only begs desperately for reassurance that they will be reunited in heaven, and Dimmesdale cannot give it to her. Hester remains unfulfilled, more a twisted and scarred relic of sin than a tragic heroine.

There is still one significant group of people within the Puritan populace which must be mentioned. There were spectators at Dimmesdale's confession who denied it all: there had been no mark, no confession, only a spectacular display of humility. These are the purest Puritans who failed to be a part of that great heart of humanity because they are so tied to their dogmas. They are slaves of the drive of the Puritan mind to maintain the validity of its simple allegory of human guilt. Membership in the Puritan community, after all, was based on the ability of that community to judge by external signs the interior consciences of men. To admit the reality of such a colossal deception as the minister's was to catch a glimpse of the precarious uncertainty of the whole Puritan social and religious system. There were bound to be some who sensed and reacted to the threat posed by the minister's confession. For these people the Puritan allegorical process went inexorably on:

According to these highly respectable witnesses, the minister, conscious that he was dying,—conscious, also, that the reverence of the multitude placed him already among saints and angels,—had desired, by yielding up his breath in the arms of that fallen woman, to express to the world how utterly nugatory is the choicest of man's own righteousness. After exhausting life in his efforts for mankind's spiritual good, he had made the manner of his death a parable, in order to impress on his admirers the mighty and mournful lesson, that, in the view of Infinite Purity, we are sinners all alike. (259)

Hawthorne strikes the same subtly ironic note here that he struck in describing the sermon at the end of Hester's hours on the scaffold. In both moments it is possible to sense the depths of Hawthorne's understanding of Puritanism, but also his understanding of humanity itself, which is able to go on quietly but persistently driving the most profoundly complex agonies of the individual conscience into the simple ethical patterns of a social code.

Hawthorne steps forward once more at the story's end, though his presence was never totally obscured at any point in the novel. Here again he is not just the story-teller who has presented the tale, but the artist-thinker who has suffered the story.

We have thrown all the light we could acquire upon the portent, and would gladly, now that it has done its office, erase its deep print out of our own brain; where long meditation has fixed it in very undesirable distinctness. (259)

As one who has both told and suffered through the story, Hawthorne, not surprisingly, emerges with a moral somewhat different from the one with which he had begun: "Be true! Be true! Be true! Show freely to the world, if not your worst, yet some trait whereby the worst may be inferred!" (260). He has not lost his hold on the principle of the sanctity of the heart, but in "A Flood of Sunshine" he gave that principle a kind of ultimate test. He submitted himself and us as fully as possible to the experience of freedom and new life which Hester held out. He created, cooperated to the full with her eloquent rhetoric. Ultimately, however he found both Hester and the principle limited and incomplete. Both fail in a fundamental relationship with reality. Hawthorne has given free play as well to the diffuse but inexorable power of nature. That too he tested to the full in the forest scene. Nature is an aspect of reality which will ultimately revenge itself on man if he fails to recognize its power, as it revenges itself on Dimmesdale and eventually on Puritanism. Still, even nature is but a vague and uncertain beacon.

There has been a refinement of Hawthorne's meaning, a modification of the principle which he set out to test in his allegory. Morality must be more than respect for the sanctity of the human heart, or rather one must respect it in all its dimensions by being ultimately and in all things true. In this very limited sense one can say that there is a moral lesson in *The Scarlet Letter*. This cuts in all directions, at Chillingworth, at Hester, at Dimmesdale, at Hawthorne himself and his own highly emotional commitment to the sanctity of the heart.

Perhaps, after our own critical journey through the novel and the forest of criticism which continues to grow up around it, we may be forced to return to the words of one of Hawthorne's earlier and better critics for our conclusion. George E. Woodberry finds Hawthorne almost as blind to the positive values of Puritanism as Hawthorne finds Puritanism blind to the values of the human heart. In emptying Puritanism of its Christian values Hawthorne has distorted "not so much the Puritan ideal—which were a little matter—but the spiritual life itself."[52] And so Hawthorne concludes with an ultimate and despairing contradiction: It may even be true that hatred and love are at bottom the same. "In the spiritual world, the old physician and the minister—mutual victims as they have been—may, unawares, have found their earthly stock of hatred and antipathy transmuted into golden love." (260-261)

In a kind of coda, we return to Hester. She has never been freed of the scar of the letter. When she returns from Europe to the settlement, she resumes it. She does gain a certain perspective, a historical perspective like Hawthorne's.[53] Still it is radically incomplete. Hester dies in sorrow and is buried separately from her love "as if the dust of the two sleepers had no right to mingle." (264)

NOTES

[1] References in parenthesis are to *The Scarlet Letter* (Ohio State University Press, 1962).
[2] Harry R. Warfel, "Metaphysical Ideas in *The Scarlet Letter*," *CE* 24 (Mar., 1963), 422.
[3] For a study of traditional symbolic meanings for all the plants involved in this scene and in *The Scarlet Letter* as a whole, see Grace Pleasant Wellborn, "Plant Lore and *The Scarlet Letter*," *SFQ* 27 (June, 1963), 160-167.

[4] Edwin Honig, *op. cit.*, p. 72, calls the rosebush a "threshold symbol." He does not take into account the fact that it is a member of a symbolic pair. Besides, the "threshold" of *The Scarlet Letter* is "The Custom-House," and there it is the letter itself which acts as the "threshold symbol."

[5] Roy R. Male, Jr., "'From the Innermost Germ': The Organic Principle in Hawthorne's Fiction," *ELH* 20 (1953), 218-236, draws out this symbolic contrast as an antithesis between the organic and the mechanical. The relationship of this symbolic pair to the development of the novel as a whole is elaborated and deepened in Charles Feidelson, Jr., "The Scarlet Letter," *Hawthorne Centenary Essays, op. cit.*, pp. 49-50. Much of my own analysis depends on the insights of Professor Feidelson. Hyatt Howe Waggoner's very schematic elaboration of the relation of these symbols to the novel as a whole in "Nathaniel Hawthorne: The Cemetery, the Prison, and the Rose," *UKCR* 14 (Spring, 1948), 176-190, seems forced.

[6] *The Text of the Spiritual Exercises of Saint Ignatius*, (Fourth Edition, revised; Westminster, Md.: The Newman Bookshop, 1943), p. 20 and *passim*. The literary use of this meditation technique has been studied by Louis L. Martz in *The Poetry of Meditation: A Study in English Religious Literature of the Seventeenth Century* (Paper; New Haven: Yale University Press, 1962), pp. 25-32.

[7] Darrell Abel, "Hawthorne's Dimmesdale: Fugitive from Wrath," *NCF* 11 (Sept., 1956), 82: "Hawthorne's narrative does not have the dramatic contuity of a moving picture; it has the static consecutiveness of a series of lantern slides, with interspersed commentary." Arlin Turner, "Hawthorne's Literary Borrowings," *PMLA* 51 (1936), 543-562, attributes this to the influence of Sir Walter Scott.

[8] Allen Austin, "Satire and Theme in *The Scarlet Letter*," *PQ* 41 (Apr., 1962), p. 508, says that Hawthorne's satire is directed against the Puritan elite, not the common people. As a matter of fact, Hawthorne makes no distinction between them in the beginning. Only gradually, as the story unfolds, do the Puritan common people come to be identified with the "great heart of humanity," while the Puritan leaders remain trapped in their dogmatism. This evolution of the common people is noted by Harry R. Warfel, *op. cit.*, p. 421.

[9] R. W. B. Lewis, "The Tactics of Sanctity," *op. cit.*, p. 275. It would be too difficult to sort out the places where this essay has pointed the way for my own analysis. For instance, p. 276: "The crucial point is this: that the meaning with which every minute of the action in *The Scarlet Letter* is charged is never quite the meaning assigned to it by the characters involved; nor could it be. For surrounding the meanings so confidently attributed to events and relationships by the magistrates and the clergymen, the matrons and the maidens, is the creative play of Hawthorne's historical imagination."

[10] Yvor Winters, *In Defense of Reason* (Third Edition, paper; Denver: Alan Swallow, n.d.), p. 161, notes that "according to the doctrine of predestination, if we interpret it reasonably, Hester merely gave evidence, in committing adultery that she had always been one of the damned." Winters goes on to say that the Puritans still treated such persons, for example, as the witches, as though they had wilfully abandoned the ways of God; this illogicality is what allows for the element of drama.

[11] Richard Poirier, *A World Elsewhere* (New York: Oxford University Press, 1966), p. 32, connects the non-realistic dialogue of Hawthorne with his own thesis that American authors as a group do not write realistic fiction but create an alternative environment, a "world elsewhere." The "dialogue" in such novels is really monologue or soliloquy. F. O. Matthiessen, *op. cit.*, p. 206,

is reminded by Hawthorne's highly artificial style of Yeats's remark that whenever language has been the instrument of controversy it inevitably grows abstract. Both of these insights supplement the explanation given here: the reason for Hawthorne's style is the allegorical form in which he writes.

12 Yvor Winters, *op. cit.,* p. 159, explains this tension within Puritanism: "Whereas the wholly Calvinistic Puritan denied the value of the evidence of character and behavior as signs of salvation, and so precluded the possibility of their becoming allegorical symbols . . . it became customary in Massachusetts to regard as evidence of salvation the decision of the individual to enter the Church and lead a moral life." The history of this development is told in Edmund S. Morgan, *Visible Saints: The History of a Puritan Idea* (Paper; Ithaca, New York: Cornell University Press, 1965).

13 Yvor Winters, *op. cit.,* p. 164: "Now in examining Hawthorne, we are concerned with two historical centers: that of the first generation of Puritans in New England, in which occurs the action of *The Scarlet Letter;* and that of the post-Unitarian and romantic intellectuals, in which was passed the life of Hawthorne."

14 Perry Miller, "From Edwards to Emerson," *Errand into the Wilderness* ("Harper Torchbooks," paper; New York: Harper and Row, Publishers, 1964), p. 192.

15 Northrop Frye, *Anatomy of Criticism: Four Essays* (Princeton, New Jersey: Princeton University Press, 1957), p. 107, says that ritual is the social expression of dream; his elaboration of that insight, on pp. 119-120, is more far-reaching than is necessary for our purposes here.

16 My debt is obvious here to Francis Fergusson, *The Idea of a Theater* ("Doubleday Anchor Books," paper; Garden City, New York: Doubleday and Company, Inc., 1953).

17 Charles Feidelson, "The Scarlet Letter," *op. cit.:* The Puritan allegory is not *the* allegory of the book, but only a part of a larger, more ambiguous allegory which is Hawthorne's. Hester calls the Puritan allegory into question, but Puritanism contains within itself the latent seed of antinomianism. Her affirmation of freedom dominates the book; but her freedom is eventually unachieved. Richard Poirier, *op. cit.,* p. 115, recognizes that Hawthorne is engaged in revealing the limits of the Puritan allegory, but he too rapidly assumes, with D. H. Lawrence, that Hawthorne submits to orthodox moral standards. For another interpretation of the double allegory of the story see Lauriat Lane, Jr., "Allegory and Character and *The Scarlet Letter,*" *ESQ,* No. 25 (Fourth Quarter, 1961), pp. 13-16: "Pearl, Chillingworth, and the whole external world of *The Scarlet Letter* are parts of a moral-psychological allegory of the state of Hester's and Dimmesdale's souls. In this sense, Hester and Dimmesdale inhabit a literal world whose actualities allegorize their own inner worlds of conscience and spirit and salvation or damnation."

18 *Op. cit.,* p. 88.

19 "The Norm of Character in the English Gothic Novel," given at the English Institute, Columbia University, September 6, 1967. This is said in somewhat different form in Richard Poirier's *A World Elsewhere, op. cit.,* p. 113: What Hawthorne investigates is the allegorizing tendencies at work in the consciousness of his characters. Hart's insight may be both an explanation of the reaction of Alexander Cowie and a refutation of it. Cowie, *op. cit.,* p. 349, complains that: "The major characters in Hawthorne's novels are generally endowed with an initial realism which falls into shadow in the progress of the story." Cowie betrays his own commitment to realism on p. 350: "The

most real characters are likely to be the least important in the action—Silas Foster in *The Blithedale Romance,* Uncle Venner in *The House of the Seven Gables.*"

[20] Darrel Abel, "The Devil in Boston," *PQ* 32 (Oct., 1953), 366-381, without using this particular passage, considers Chilingworth an example of goodness perverted rather than of evil incarnate.

[21] Such a force could very well have its origin in the unconscious. This is Frederick Crews' explanation of all three of the main characters, *op. cit.,* p. 139.

[22] Roy R. Male, "Hawthorne's Allegory of Guilt and Redemption," *ESQ,* No. 25 (Fourth Quarter, 1961), p. 16: "By its very nature the allegorical technique tends to exemplify 'how an influence beyond our control lays its strong hand on every deed which we do, and weaves its consequences into an iron band of necessity.'"

[23] Charles Feidelson, "The Scarlet Letter," *op. cit.,* p. 47: "As administrators of the code, the ministers and magistrats on the balcony have no concrete human existence for themselves or others, and they have no perception of the concrete reality of Hester on the scaffold. . . . They see only the abstract adulteress."

[24] Seymour L. Gross, " 'Solitude, and Love, and Anguish': The Tragic Design of *The Scarlet Letter,*" *CLAJ* 3 (Mar., 1960), 154-165, emphasizes the separateness of the moral universes in which Hester and Dimmesdale live, but he falls prey to the radical dichotomy between realistic characters and allegorical characters with clear conceptual meanings. The point of my analysis is that the meanings of both Hester and Dimmesdale shift and evolve. Bruce Ingham Granger, "Arthur Dimmesdale as Tragic Hero," *NCF* 19 (Sept., 1964), 197-203, claims that Dimmesdale alone never functions symbolically and that he represents Every-Christian. The position of those who make Dimmesdale the hero of the book will be examined toward the end of this analysis.

[25] William Bysshe Stein, *Hawthorne's Faust: A Study of the Devil Archetype* (Gainesville: University of Florida Press, 1953).

[26] Jane Lundblad, *Nathaniel Hawthorne and the Tradition of Gothic Romance* ("Essays and Studies on American Language and Literature," IV; Cambridge, Mass.: Harvard University Press, 1946), remains on the surface of Gothic. Leslie Fiedler's discussion of the Gothic is more satisfactory. See, for example, the citation on p. 79 of my analysis of "The Custom-House." Fiedler's discussion of the Gothic in Hawthorne is on pp. 131-140 of *Love and Death, op. cit.*

[27] Marius Bewley, "Hawthorne and the Deeper Psychology," *Mandrake,* Vol. 2, p. 367: "The interest we feel in Hester Prynne is of an essentially different kind from the interest we feel in Isabel Archer. In the last analysis Hawthorne is not interested in Hester's private drama. She exists magnificently in the art as the focus of tangled moral forces, but she is herself as much of a symbol as the Scarlet Letter which she wears on her breast." The positive statement of Hester's symbolic value is right, but why is it necessary to say that Hawthorne is not interested in her private drama? Frederick Crews points out the essential fallacy in Bewley's understanding of "the deeper psychology" in *Sins of the Fathers, op. cit.,* p. 16: "If she [Hester] is a more schematic figure than Isabel, her motives are deeper and better known to us. It is precisely because Hawthorne is not afraid to schematize, to stress underlying patterns of compulsion rather than superficial eccentricities, that he is able to explore 'the depths of our common nature.'" Bewley is right in saying that Hawthorne

tells us more about man, less about men (p. 367), but wrong in going on to say that "Hawthorne's interest turns its back on the psychological for the sake of squarely confronting the moral."

[28] Many critics have adverted to the problem, here symbolically expressed, of the artist and society, but Hawthorne himself does not develop it. It is rather a part of the general picture of Puritanism as a religion at war with itself. The paradoxical flamboyance of Puritan taste will appear more clearly later in the novel and join itself to several other motifs which we can for the moment call "the force of nature."

[29] F. O. Matthiessen, *op. cit.*, p. 278: "She is worth dissecting as the purest type of Spenserian characterization, which starts with abstract qualities and hunts for their proper embodiment; worth murdering, most modern readers of fiction would hold, since the tedious reiteration of what she stands for betrays Hawthorne at his most barren." Darrel Abel, "Hawthorne's Pearl: Symbol and Character," *ELH* 18 (Mar., 1951), 66, concurs.

[30] Waggoner, in "The Cemetery, the Prison, and the Rose," *op. cit.*, p. 185, argues more reasonably that "contemporary psycho-analysis throws much light on the reasons for the perversity of this child reared without a father and with only imperfect and mixed love for her mother."

[31] Yvor Winters' allegorical interpretation of this scene, *op. cit.*, p. 166, is far-fetched: "The portraits are obviously intended as an apology for the static portraits in the book, as an illustration of the principle of simplification by distance and by generalization; the new armor, on the other hand, is the new faith which brought the Puritans to New England, . . ." He is closer to what Hawthorne himself has made clear in his interpretation of Governor Bellingham: "Governor Bellingham, in his combination of legal training with military prowess, is representative of his fellow colonists, who displayed in a remarkable degree a capacity to act with great strength and with absolutely simple directness upon principles so generalized as scarcely to be applicable to any particular moral problem, which mastered moral difficulties not by understanding them, but by crushing them out."

[32] Note how close Hawthorne's Chillingworth is to the appraisal of the physician of those times given by a modern-day historian, Wallace Notestein, *The English People on the Eve of Colonization: 1603-1630* ("Harper Torchbooks," paper; New York: Harper and Row, 1962), p. 105: "Undoubtedly physicians were looked upon by many, and notably by the ignorant, as rather queer, unearthly people, who dealt in a kind of magic, an attitude which medical men did not always discourage. Moreover they were not as a class greatly concerned with religion. It was observed that the more skill they had, the less devout they were. Too much they attributed to natural causes and not enough to Providence. Such men were always a little suspect. They were, I think, often outsiders, not quite an integral part of the natural good fellowship."

[33] Terence Martin, *Nathaniel Hawthorne*, (New York: Twayne Publishers, Inc., 1965), p. 116.

[34] Bewley, *The Eccentric Design*, (New York: Columbia University Press, 1963), p. 167: "There are points at which the guilt of society almost seems to absorb the personal guilt of Hester. But such a resolution would be highly uncharacteristic of Hawthorne, and in the end we find the problem complicated by certain factors in Hester's own mind and character which suggest that inherent moral flaws have found nutriment in the social penalty under which she has had to suffer." A little further on Bewley defines these flaws as "the development of a speculative turn of mind which Hawthorne, to a degree not

often recognized today, found sinful, and imputable to Hester alone." Giovanni Gullace, "Péché et pécheurs dans *La Lettre Ecarlate et Le Faune de Marbre*," *Etudes Anglaises* 15 (April-June, 1962), 113-131, follows what is almost a tradition in French criticism, and considers Hester free of guilt because she does not share Dimmesdale's Puritan conscience. The distortion within her, according to Gullace, is fully the responsibility of the community.

[35] Darrel Abel, in "Hawthorne's Dimmesdale," *op. cit.*, is one of the few critics who sees Hester's denial of the letter as a significant action.

[36] *Hawthorne as Myth-Maker, op. cit.*, p. 11.

[37] William H. Nolte, "Hawthorne's Dimmesdale: A Small Man Gone Wrong," *NEQ* 38 (June, 1965), 168-186, infuses his dissatisfaction with an attitude of impatience with those who disagree. They merely betray their own moral absolutism.

[38] Frederic I. Carpenter, "Scarlet A Minus," *CE* 5 (Jan., 1944), 178: "Most obviously, Hawthorne imposed a moralistic 'Conclusion' upon the drama which his characters had acted. But the artistic and moral falsity of this does not lie in its didacticism or in the personal intrusion of the author, for these were the literary conventions of the age. Rather it lies in the contradiction between the author's moralistic comments and the earlier words and actions of his characters. Having created living protagonists, Hawthorne sought to impose his own will and judgment upon them from the outside."

[39] Edward H. Davidson, "Hawthorne and the Pathetic Fallacy," *JEGP* 54 (October, 1955), p. 488.

[40] He has recreated, if less directly, the world of *The Faerie Queene*, as well, specifically the wandering of Una and the Red Cross Knight in the forest. See Randall Stewart, "Hawthorne and *The Faerie Queene*," *PQ* 12 (1933), 196-206.

[41] Hester is almost a perfect example of the heroine whom Denis de Rougemont describes in *L'Amour et L'Occident* ("Le Monde en 10/18"; Paris: Union Generale d'Editions, n.d., original copyright, 1939), p. 31: "En vérité, comme tous les grands amants, ils se sentent ravis 'par delà le bien et le mal', dans une sorte de transcendance de nos communes conditions, dans un absolu indicible, incompatible avec les lois du monde, mais qu'ils éprouvent comme plus *réel que ce monde*. La fatalité qui les presse, et à laquelle ils s'abandonnent en gémissant, supprime l'opposition du bien et du mal; elle les conduit même audelà de l'origine de toutes valeurs morales, au-delà du plaisir et de la souffrance, audelà du domaine où l'on distingue, et où les contraires s'excluent."

[42] To look upon *The Scarlet Letter* strictly as a story of isolation from society is to fail to see all of its dimensions. This is the difficulty with the interpretation of Lawrence S. Hall in his *Hawthorne, Critic of Society* ("Yale Studies in English," Vol. 99; New Haven: Yale University Press, 1944). One immediate result is the failure to see the full significance of Pearl. Hall, p. 168, says that she "stands for Hester's obligation to society." J. W. Mathews, "Hawthorne and the Chain of Being," *MLQ* 18 (Dec., 1957), 283-294, broadens the thesis slightly by speaking of isolation from one's place in both nature and society. Certainly Hawthorne believes that there is no real solution to any human problem without some kind of integration with society, though he is not able to say how one is to find such a society. One must be true both to oneself and to society. Hester is neither. Neither is Dimmesdale. W. Stacy Johnson, "Sin and Salvation in Hawthorne," *The Hibbert Journal* 50 (Oct., 1951), 39-47, believes that the reconciliation with society which takes place "on the scaffold is a complete vision of salvation: final salvation for Dimmesdale and a regenerative experience of salvation's way for Hester and Pearl.

The way is through communion, expressed in love and honesty." (44) This, it seems to me, elevates reconciliation to society to a position far beyond the one that Hawthorne assigns it. It certainly goes far beyond the very limited "salvation" Hawthorne is willing to allow his characters.

[43] Chester E. Eisinger, "Pearl and the Puritan Heritage," *CE* 12 (Mar., 1951), 323-329, calls Pearl an old-fashioned Puritan child. The dominant fact about her is her kinship with nature as the Puritans defined nature. Granting this, it must be noted that Pearl is not the same as nature, Puritan or Hawthornesque. When nature smiles on Hester and Dimmesdale, Pearl frowns. This is not the Puritan conception of wild, amoral nature. Roy R. Male, *Hawthorne's Tragic Vision* (Austin: University of Texas Press, 1957), p. 94, interprets Pearl as the visible embodiment of truth about sin, one who rejects all half-truths, including those of the Puritans. Even some members of the romantic school of interpretation accept this meaning of Pearl. L. Dhaleine, *Nathaniel Hawthorne, sa vie et son ouvre* (Paris: Hachette & Cie., 1905), p. 161, says that "Perle est celui de nos personages qui ressent le mieux cette influence bienfaisante (de la vérité rédemptrice)." His sense of "truth," however, is closer to the idea of sincerity unspoiled by social conventions. Even D. H. Lawrence, *Studies in Classic American Literature* ("Anchor Books", paper; Garden City, New York: Doubleday and Company, Inc., 1955) speaks of Pearl's function as principle of truth, p. 107: "If you have brought forth, spawned, a young malevolence, be sure there is a rampant falseness in the world against which this malevolence must be turned. Falseness has to be bitten and bitten, till it is bitten to death. Hence Pearl."

[44] "Form and Content in *The Scarlet Letter*," *NEQ* 17 (1944), 25-55. Malcolm Cowley in "Five Acts of *The Scarlet Letter*," *CE* 19 (Oct., 1957), 11-16, analyses the structure of the story according to the divisions of the drama, but does not thereby prejudice the allegorical nature of the story. Hawthorne, according to Cowley, learned to work in small forms and to present his subjects as moral essays or allegorical pictures rather than as continuously moving narratives.

[45] *Hawthorne, op. cit.,* p. 109. Two of those who follow James: Robert F. Haugh, "The Second Secret in *The Scarlet Letter*," *CE* 17 (February, 1956), 269-271, says that the action of the book begins when Hester reveals Chillingworth's identity, because only then does Dimmesdale have a visible evil against which to take a stand. But what of the rest of the novel? Franz Link, *Die Erzählkunst Nathaniel Hawthornes* (Heidelberg: C. Winter, 1962), orients his whole analysis around Dimmesdale because Dimmesdale changes and Hester doesn't.

[46] "*The Scarlet Letter* as a Love Story," *PMLA* 77 (September, 1962), 425-435.

[47] This is the position of Ernest Sandeen in the article quoted above. Accordingly, there is no "conversion" from one self into another, but a new synthesis of the man of conscience and the man of passion. His confession is both a public confession of sin and a bearing witness to the power of passion. Hester represents the Western tradition of the "grand passion." Dimmesdale is the central character because the issue between Hester's commitment to the "grand passion" and the town's commitment to rigid morality comes to a focus in him. The resolution of the struggle "reveals how Hawthorne has shifted the point of view from which the story of true love is usually told to a more impartial perspective" (p. 434). The point I would like to make, over and above this, is that some of the shifting takes place within the novel itself. Hawthorne

tested out Hester's idea of love and found it wanting. Finally, Dimmesdale's final fear casts doubt on Sandeen's contention that he arrives at a point of resolution. Frederick Crews, *Sins of the Fathers, op. cit.*, rejects the arguments of those who find Hester to be the moral ideal of the book; but he rejects, as well, those who identify Hawthorne's point of view with Dimmesdale's. Crews settles for a conjecture that Hawthorne is ironic, neither romantic nor orthodox. At any rate, both Crews and Sandeen see the election-day sermon as a very ambiguous release of passion.

48 *The Eccentric Design, op. cit.*, 163.

49 Harry R. Warfel, in "Metaphysical Ideas in *The Scarlet Letter*," *op. cit.*, speculates that the rewritten sermon has a hidden meaning for Hester, according to which Hester is right, old laws and institutions must be upset by free individuals.

50 Thomas F. Walsh, "Dimmesdale's Election Sermon," *ESQ,* No. 44 (Third Quarter, 1966), pp. 64-66, notes that historically the theme of Dimmesdale's sermon was standard for the times, but uses it as a sign of Dimmesdale's genuine conversion; it is his recognition of the divine election of both himself and all New England.

51 Darrel Abel, "Hawthorne's Pearl," *op. cit.*

52 *Nathaniel Hawthorne* (Boston: Houghton Mifflin Company, 1902), pp. 202-203.

53 R. W. B. Lewis, "The Tactics of Sanctity," *op. cit.*, p. 277. Both Hugo McPherson, *op. cit.*, p. 186, and Marjorie Elder, *Nathaniel Hawthorne: Transcendental Symbolist* (Ohio University Press, 1969), p. 126, credit Hester with full insight into the meaning of the letter at the time of her return. Hawthorne's conclusion, however, doesn't seem to bear them out.

Allegory and History

Typology

One of the most striking aspects of Hawthorne's writing seems, to a theoretical eye, totally at odds with the allegorical tradition. This is Hawthorne's deep involvement with history: not theory of history, but the details of his country's past. Because allegory has traditionally been concerned with the timeless moral realities of human nature, history and allegory do not, it would seem, belong together. Western culture, however, has absorbed at least one very significant attempt to unite history and allegory, or rather, more precisely, to place the realities of history in some kind of relationship with the timeless, whether God or some other trans-historical reality, in order to give meaning to the concrete but passing event.

This attempt had its origins among the Jews, who based their religious life on the experience of God's intervention in their history rather than on the fertile and destructive cycles of nature.[1] What they saw in these events was God's fidelity to the people he had molded and the promise of a glorious future. Gradually the "future" became an ultimate future, an end-time after history when God would fulfill his promises.[2]

This effort to remain faithful to the unique realities of historical time reached its climax when the writers of the New Testament saw the coming of Christ as the decisive event toward which all the events of Jewish history had been moving. The New Testament is the literary record of this perception, and it constitutes a complete re-reading of the Old Testament in the light of the coming of Christ. But this historical insight rapidly

155

proved incomplete. Although Christ had fulfilled the Jewish eschatological expectations in the eyes of these early Christians, it gradually became clear that history was not over. As a result, the religious imagination was once again cast forward to another awaited *pleroma* when all things would be restored in Christ. The events of his earthly life, then, became a central point between the past and this new end-time in the future. These three moments, then, the period of the Old Testament, the life of Christ, and the time of the second coming, make the configuration of what is known to us as biblical typology.

In the effort to make Jewish and Christian history one history by making the Law and the Prophets one book with the Gospels and Epistles, the New Testament writers gave only indications of the relationship between the two sets of writings. Some of these indications were explicit, but very brief, almost buried in the urgency of the Gospel message.[3] Others were long Midrashic meditations on the parallels between the life of Christ and various central figures of the Jewish past.[4] These preliminary indications were taken up into the biblical commentaries of the Church Fathers and vitally continued into the Middle Ages, when the Bible was read in terms of the famous four-fold sense. The literary significance of this effort has been studied by Erich Auerbach, especially in his "Figura."[5]

American literature, of course, post-dates by years the vital interplay of theology and culture which culminated in Dante, Auerbach's climactic example of the literary fruitfulness of "figura" or typology. But the tradition of typological interpretation did not die with the Reformation. And since the Reformation was in a certain sense a broadening of the base of Christianity, a serious extension of the Christian life beyond monastery walls, and an almost desperate attempt to fight off a returning wave of paganism by a Christianization of secular life, it is not surprising to learn that a concept so recondite as typology should have entered almost pervasively into the thinking and writing of the American Puritans. Perhaps they found in it a way of compensating for the confined severity of their lives, giving them as it did a significance great as all history. For them, their exodus to America was the beginning of the realization of that final end-time. America has been from the beginning a country obsessed by the exciting possibility of being the final kingdom of God on earth.

But the dogmatic coherence of Puritanism was short-lived in America. And the question arises: In the light of the fact that the Puritans were so important to the development of American literature, can one identify vestigial remnants of their ways of thinking, their formal habits of mind, in spite of the death of their dogmas. This is the question to which Ursula Brumm addressed herself in her study: *American Thought and Religious Typology.*[6]

According to this study, the Puritans very quickly stretched the concept and use of typology beyond the strict function it fulfilled in the interpretation of Scripture. Very rapidly the idea of *type* lost the quality which was specific to it, its claim to be rooted in history. By the time of the last great Puritan, Jonathan Edwards, the concept of type had become merely another word for symbol and allegory. Nevertheless Hawthorne, coming long after Edwards and the decline of the Puritan faith in the meaning of history, is committed both to history and to the formulation of meaning through history. The question then is: has Hawthorne, the heir of the Puritans, inherited a vision of history in any way related to the Puritan or Medieval theory of typology?

There have been some interesting recent studies of Hawthorne's historical vision, among which Gretchen Graf Jordan's comes closest to attributing to Hawthorne a typological ground of thought:

> In broad terms, he saw the history of American culture as a continuous growth out of Anglo-Saxon Protestantism. He looked upon the first Puritans as earnest and severe fighters for their own liberty who, by reason of that severity and intolerance, established a moral law and the beginning of a new civilization in the primitive forests of the New World. He viewed the American Revolution as the flowering of a gradual growth of the Puritan principle of liberty. Finally, he thought of the evolutionary process as still going on in America, and hopefully discerned in the future a still wider spread of Christian love and democratic brotherhood.[7]

Hawthorne's philosophy can thus be expressed in a proportion:

the Puritans are to the development of "the universal brother-
hood of man in a democracy"[8] as the men of the Old Testament
were to the new revelation in Christ. Miss Jordan does not
relate this historical vision, however, to the typological tradition
of the Puritans, but rather to Hawthorne's acquaintance with the
contemporary German "Higher Critics" of the Bible. The evidence she adduces for this attribution is, however, tenuous:

> Hawthorne probably first encountered this complex of ideas
> through the work of certain American scholars who, in the
> late 1820's and 1830's, were insisting on a recognition of
> German contributions to Biblical studies. Whether or not
> Hawthorne yet knew any of these men personally, he un-
> doubtedly followed their arguments in the journals, particularly
> in the *Christian Examiner,* which in "The Old Manse" he
> claims to have "rummaged."[9]

Perhaps Miss Jordan's "undoubtedly" is more defensive than real.
Contemporary German biblical criticism would have had to penetrate rather deeply into Hawthorne's way of looking at America
to produce the kind of pattern Miss Jordan finds. And yet we
have already seen, in our survey of "The Old Manse" the con-
tempt with which Hawthorne regarded the theological writings
he discovered there.

Still, Miss Jordan's analysis of "The Bell's Biography" yields
insights into Hawthorne's historical vision which are very per-
suasive. Her discussion, for instance, of the irony of history
rings true:

> Hence Hawthorne's historical characters seldom arrive at any
> spiritual insight. They are all too often blind and deaf to the
> real future and even to the significance of their own acts.
> They live and die for their own conscious purposes. Some are
> sure that those purposes have been accomplished and that
> God has revealed His purpose as being at one with theirs. But
> no more than the heroes of Greek tragedy can they see that
> God is using them for a purpose not their own. As more recent
> critics have pointed out, Hawthorne several times remarks
> that almost no consciously planned social action has ever
> really succeeded in the way that its proponents intended. Man
> proposes and God disposes.[10]

A final judgment on Miss Jordan's perception of a unified historical myth in Hawthorne will have to await the complete study of Hawthorne's historical tales and sketches on which she was working at the time of her article.

What the present study of Hawthorne as allegorist has tended to show is that Hawthorne examined the secular faith in democracy from multiple angles of vision and concluded that the evolution toward democracy in America was right with the movement of history, though shot through with psychological consequences of guilt and ambiguity. It has also tended to show that Hawthorne was interested not only in the movement of American history, but also looked upon that history as in some way, usually not explicitly elaborated, a symbol for the universal strivings of men. A unified historical myth is not necessary for the inspection and testing out of these problems. It has not yet been proven

> that Hawthorne carefully plotted the course of American history, generation by generation, that he illuminated each of these generations by at least one tale, and that none of these tales could be lifted out of its own generation without violating its essential meaning.[11]

Johannes Kjorven's "Hawthorne and the Significance of History" is a study with a more Platonic, less Biblical emphasis:

> To Hawthorne the past dramatizes and makes vital one's connection with the eternal in the present and with the universal verities.[12]

Kjorven differs rightly from Miss Jordan in emphasizing the fact that Hawthorne felt free to modify the facts of history in order to gain significance. What Hawthorne needs is not the facts but the sense of a vital historical tradition which "sifts and winnows the historical material and preserves the general image of history."[13] Kjorven, then, denies Hawthorne's interest in history as an end in itself as well as any interest in making history " 'meaningful' in terms of a pattern or valid laws of continuity, or in terms of changing human aspirations and values which are temporarily relevant and valid within the historical process."[14]

Kjorven thinks that for Hawthorne history is always a means to
an eternal truth, a position that must be carefully qualified. But
he does not fall into the trap of making Hawthorne a naive
allegorist. Hawthorne does not arrive at his truths through simple logic: "The poetic truth grows out of Hawthorne's sense of
a complete rhythm of experience."[15]

> Having once gone through this rhythm of experience and
> acquired a new understanding of the march of history, one
> knows that the " 'past, dismal as it seems, shall fling no gloom
> upon the future. To give it its due importance we must think
> of it but as an anecdote in our Eternity.' "[16]

An interesting aspect of Kjorven's thinking about Hawthorne is
that he seems to be unaware of the breakdown of a publicly
accepted set of values in Hawthorne's time:

> Therefore the allegorical view of history remains the stabilizing
> factor which he applies to his artistic vision. As allegory
> depends on a scheme of publicly accepted values, it does not
> blur the lines of demarcation in the moral conflict. Symbolism
> enriches and makes the significant historical episode more
> complex, while allegory defines it in the light of a long tra-
> dition.[17]

Perhaps this explains his sense that in some unexplained way
Hawthorne does commit himself to the demonstration of eternal
verities.

We come finally to Ursula Brumm who alone has studied
the Puritan typological tradition and related it to Hawthorne.
She too argues that Hawthorne deals with eternal verities, but
she finally decides he is neither allegorist, symbolist, nor typolo-
gist but emblematist. As emblematist, Hawthorne sees meanings
in things and in tableaux, but does not develop them into allegorical structures.

But Miss Brumm assumes a very narrow definition of allegory
and supposes that the "pure allegorist" develops his story from
an abstraction and not from the conceptual apprehension of a
human problem in a concrete situation. She betrays the narrow-
ness of her definition of allegory in a later context when she

states that the multiplicity of meaning in Hawthorne's symbols makes him unfit for flat, univocal allegory.[18] Flat, univocal allegory is merely naive allegory. Miss Brumm virtually ignores the ambiguity which is intrinsic to sophisticated allegory and seems to exclude the possibility—conceded to writers in all other literary genres—of reformulating and thereby revitalizing the genre of allegory.

Miss Brumm's reluctance to call Hawthorne an allegorist, though it betrays an unnecessarily reduced sense of the form, is based on an accurate perception of Hawthorne's thematic intent:

In Hawthorne the reality of thought, idea, and imagination continually interpenetrates physical reality to such an extent that ideas, thought, supersensual things, and even chimeras can exert influence just like real, palpable things.[19]

But it is precisely this desire to emphasize the reality of the non-palpable which characterizes Romantic and post-Romantic allegory. This is, perhaps, the basic insight involved in Edwin Honig's pervasive efforts to connect Kafka with the medieval allegorical tradition. The aspects of Hawthorne which, Miss Brumm feels, exclude him from the ranks of the world's allegorists are actually basic to any allegorical enterprise which post-dates the Romantic movement.

Miss Brumm, having herself traced the very rapid decline of authentic typology in American literature, rightly considers it no more than an influence on Hawthorne. As a matter of fact, the difference between typology and allegory is, like the difference between realism and allegory, a relative matter. We may define the extremes: The relationship between the raising of the brazen serpent during the Exodus and the lifting of Christ on the cross, a relationship between two historical events, is typological. The relationship between the Red Cross Knight and holiness, a relationship between an abstract quality and an imaginary person, is allegorical. But both allegory and typology are ways of binding together meaning and event in a literary work. Consequently they may flow into one another, influence one another in an infinite variety of ways.[20] Still it is important to recognize that Hawthorne does not just create allegorical scenes and symbols, but allegories; the typological tradition simply opened to him the possibilities for making allegories of history.

Taking the Gray Champion as Hawthorne's most explicit example of a "type" we may say, as does Miss Brumm,[21] that he is not an abstraction with an abstract name like "Freedom" but a concrete figure of a determined historical period. Hawthorne, we conclude, veers toward the typological. But we must also say that Hawthorne leaves his figure nameless and clearly makes him the personification of an abstract quality. That abstract quality is not one of the "eternal" virtues of the Aristotelian or Medieval canon, but rather the spirit of New England, the spirit of a historical movement among a small group of people during a historically delimited era, its beginning in the rise of Puritanism, its end unknowable yet. We automatically understand, however, that the will of the Puritans to be free is not something unique in history, but typical of a universal human aspiration to freedom. The Gray Champion, then, is not a type; rather, the typological mode of thought, with its respect for historical figures, has influenced Hawthorne's creation of an allegorical personification.

One finds Miss Brumm consistently straining to magnify in Hawthorne the importance not just of Puritan thought-forms but of Puritan faith. She notes an important shift in Hawthorne from an authentic typological vision:

> God no longer fixes types and emblems peremptorily as manifestations of His will. He causes the inner working of the human heart to manifest themselves as types in earthly things.[22]

Can we say, though, that Hawthorne adverted to the role of God in the drive of the heart toward self-revelation? One is made to experience it rather as a law of the heart that for Hawthorne had little, if any, connection with religious faith. In another area Miss Brumm overstates the importance of Puritan faith in Hawthorne: The creation of allegory was, to the Puritans, blasphemous, an arrogation to man of the creative power of God. Man was rather to find the emblems that God had placed in the world around him and interpret their divine meaning.

Hawthorne, according to Miss Brumm, submitted to this Puritan restriction finding emblems rather than creating allegories:

> Hawthorne's types are not embodiments of abstract ideas which the human mind has come up with for literary purposes. Instead they are things, persons, and scenes, allegedly real or veritably real, and the writer discovers a deeper meaning expressed in them.[23]

Hawthorne didn't find the Gray Champion; he made him up, out of details from history, no doubt, but made him up nevertheless. It is, of course, infinitely curious to know what an author finds as opposed to what he creates. But it is virtually impossible to know because of the nature of knowledge itself. Perhaps the Puritans thought they were finding, not creating meaning-laden objects. But, though the objects were undoubtedly there, their meanings were the fruit of a rudimentary social creative act. Even if it were possible to concede that Hawthorne thought he was finding meanings, we would have to say that, according to all the evidence of the Notebooks, he was extraordinarily blind to his own processes of thought. His notes are a steady and lifelong witness to the conscious effort to generate meaning.

Finding meaning, it seems, can only have one intelligibility: to accept the meanings one has consciously or unconsciously derived from society. One who thinks that he does not impose meaning is one who merely accepts meaning from others. But the burden of our discussion of *The Scarlet Letter,* especially of its Custom-House introduction, indicates that the allegorical effort of Hawthorne was precisely to create: to reject the allegorical "findings" of Puritanism as arbitrary and narrow, and to create, by means of his own historical vision, a rival allegorical world, independent of both the opaque realities of the contemporary and the schematized realities of the Puritan past. Miss Brumm's emphasis on Hawthorne's "finding" of meanings makes him a Puritan anachronism and ignores his concerted effort to stand free of both his own world and of the narrow dogmas of Puritanism.

Miss Brumm's discussion of Hawthorne's view of time accumulates more evidence for making him out an allegorist. Hawthorne does not grasp time as a flow, but stops it in tableaux. In spite of what she has said about the Gray Champion, Miss Brumm here concedes that Hawthorne's characters are not historical individuals but demonstrate distinctive meanings and embody certain principles. Time, then, is cyclic, always bringing back, in new masks and costumes, the same situations, the same character types.

The House of the Seven Gables proves the most fruitful source for both Kjorven and Miss Brumm in their discussion of Hawthorne's attitude to history. In this work some kind of typology seems to have been operative: the original story of Maule's curse may be called a "type" of the story of the whole Pyncheon line;[24] the downfall of the Pyncheons illustrates the downfall of Puritanism which betrayed its mission through hunger for power, selfishness, and religious fanaticism;[25] cyclic recurrence is anchored in human moral qualities rather than divine omnipotence.[26] Here too, Miss Brumm is more justified in finding Hawthorne intermittently allegorical rather than a creator of allegorical structures. *The House of the Seven Gables,* however, does not deserve to be placed in a position of *de facto* superiority to *The Scarlet Letter.* Hawthorne's most unified and most fully realized works of fiction are some of the short tales and *The Scarlet Letter.* In these works Hawthorne created allegories based on the Puritan past as itself a symbol for the recurring problems of human existence. In *The House of the Seven Gables,* on the other hand, Hawthorne, trying too hard to bind up past and present, is in the grip of a more schematized literary form which may or may not have been the result of acquaintance with biblical typology. It would seem that the form chosen in the writing of *The Scarlet Letter* was much the more appropriate to the nature of his skill and convictions as a writer.

If Hawthorne is an allegorist, then something, it would seem, ought to be said about the truths he conveys. Kjorven finds that: "To Hawthorne the past dramatizes and makes vital one's connection with the eternal in the present and with the universal verities."[27] Miss Brumm says that history, in Hawthorne, is the time-coordinate for unchanging moral categories. Though neither critic is so rash as to say that Hawthorne formulated any of these eternal verities, a more accurate statement, it seems to me, would be a negative one. According to James K. Folsom, in *Man's Accidents and God's Purposes,* the statement would have to be purely negative: Hawthorne does not make clear moral points because he does not believe they can be made. No action can be judged in terms of an ultimate reality. No character is ever the representative of Hawthorne's view; no character has moral meaning. Folsom concludes that Hawthorne does not write allegory.[28]

It is true that in the "eschatological scene," in *The Scarlet Letter,* when the minister stands at midnight on the scaffold, Hawthorne does seem to shy away from his own vision of an ultimate truth. But his characters do have meaning, though it is rarely simple and, as with Hester, it usually undergoes a process of development. And Hawthorne does make moral judgments, in the sense that he engages in fictional speculation about moral principles and comes up with very limited conclusions. Perhaps one may feel that what Hawthorne arrives at is the "eternal problems" rather than the "eternal verities." We do recognize in "The Gray Champion" and "Howe's Masquerade" that some principles are at least historically right: they fit the movement of history and they respond to a basic human demand for self-determination. Again we have no doubt that there is something wrong and even pernicious about young Goodman Brown. Finally, we find in *The Scarlet Letter* a thoroughgoing commitment to reverence for the human heart, which in the course of the novel develops into a commitment to reverence for the whole truth about the human heart. Hawthorne is an allegorist who knows how little he knows, but does not shy away from probing for what limited truth he may uncover.

The question of "truth" in Hawthorne brings us, for a moment, to the fictional surface of Hawthorne's allegory, the question of reality and its rival explanations, the scientific and the superstitious. Miss Brumm attacks Hawthorne's technique of multiple explanations as an inconsistency of style resulting from the fact that Hawthorne was never able to reconcile the Puritan and the nineteenth-century components of his mind.[29] But again Miss Brumm attributes to orthodox Puritan dogma a power over Hawthorne's mind which none of the evidence justifies. She fails to see that Hawthorne's alternate explanations are precisely his way of breaking through the common-sense, scientifically-explainable surface of events to uncover the fact that spiritual experiences, whatever be their reality-foundation, sensible or superstitious, have real effects. "Young Goodman Brown" is the definitive demonstration of this.

Allegory and Symbolism

Though it is the more interesting question to deal with, the problem of typology in Hawthorne is probably not of very urgent critical interest. The opposition that is probably foremost in the mind of any critic who considers the possibility of calling Hawthorne an allegorist is the modern prejudice in favor of symbolism. In fact, except for a few critics who can do both, it seems impossible to like Hawthorne and at the same time call him an allegorist. A citation from Northrop Frye may be appropriate here:

> The commenting critic is often prejudiced against allegory without knowing the real reason, which is that continuous allegory prescribes the direction of his commentary, and so restricts its freedom. Hence he often urges us to read Spenser and Bunyan, for example, for the story alone and let the allegory go, meaning by that that he regards his own type of commentary as more interesting. Or else he will frame a definition of allegory that will exclude the poems he likes. Such a critic is often apt to treat all allegory as though it were naive allegory, or the translation of ideas into images.[30]

Hawthorne, as has been repeatedly shown in these analyses, employs so many of the techniques of allegory so consistently that he demands the formation of a concept of allegory which will be broad enough to include his skepticism and historical vision and accurate enough to show the essential bond of unity between him and his great medieval and renaissance predecessors. Once we have formulated such a concept and cleared away any confusion between sophisticated and naive allegory, the pressure to explain his greatness no longer requires that we group him with the symbolists. We recognize more readily that it is no impeachment of his greatness to say that he likes a degree of explicit control over the meaning of his symbols. We need no longer say, with Matthiessen, that his allegorical use of symbols "short-circuits the range of association"[31] because we know that symbols need not only be sources for an essentially limitless expanse of imaginative reverberations. Literary works of recognized validity and stature have kept symbols under the kind of conceptual control characteristic of allegory, and that type of literature did not die with the break-down of common values. It still lives because Hawthorne, among others, reformulated it and kept it alive.

Marius Bewley demonstrates a limited sense of the inadequacy of symbolism to cover all the good in literary imagery. Earlier, in "Hawthorne and 'The Deeper Psychology,' " he had said that:

> Hawthorne is not, except at his lower levels, an allegorist despite the frequency of the attribution. To a degree that Poe never achieved, although the tag has frequently been tied to him, Hawthorne is a symbolist.[32]

Behind Bewley's distinction lurks the conventional contrast between allegory and symbolism.

> We shall see how he is able to elevate the problems that confront the deeper consciousness of his characters to an impersonal level where, leaving behind the individuating characteristics of the unique and the local, they live with a growing symbolic life in the imagination of his readers.[33]

The interesting fact is that Bewley follows this very legitimate observation about Hawthorne's symbols with a thorough-going allegorical interpretation of "The Hollow of the Three Hills."

By the time of his *The Eccentric Design,* Bewley has seen that:

> the current emphasis on symbolism, and on symbolism of a particular kind, is unfortunate in two respects. It tends to draw an unnatural division in the American literary tradition, to place an important group of writers on the wrong side of sadly misplaced tracks; and, secondly, it minimizes or even denies the importance of subject matter to the symbolist artist. He is left with only the symbolizing process of his own mind for subject-matter.[34]

But this is all there is to Bewley's change of heart. He incorporates essentially the same allegorical analysis as before while continuing to deny that Hawthorne is writing allegory: "I have written elsewhere that *The Scarlet Letter* is not an allegory on the woman taken in adultery, but a subtle exploration of moral isolation in America."[35] Either he is saying that the novel is an allegory of moral isolation in America, or he is saying, and this seems more likely, that an allegory cannot be a "subtle exploration."

But at least in theory Bewley tends to minimize the distinction between allegorists and symbolists. The insistence of Scholes and Kellogg in *The Nature of Narrative* on the distinction between lyric and narrative, as well as their insight into the history of the allegory-symbolism opposition will suffice, perhaps, to conclude this discussion:

The other problem of definition which must be dealt with here is that of the frequently invoked distinction between allegory and symbolism. Forcefully established in English letters by Blake and Yeats, this invidious distinction sees symbolism as being organic, non-intellectual, pointing to some mystical connection between the mind of the poet and that unreal world which is the shaping mind or soul behind actuality, wearing what we call the "real" world as its vestment. In this essentially romantic view allegory is contrasted with symbolism as being overtly intellectual and excessively didactic, reflecting the real world in a mechanical and superficial way. But in the practice of *narrative* art (we must insist here on its separation from lyric) this distinction, whatever its absolute validity, is hardly tenable. . . . In narrative any recurring symbol, whether it is an object, a gesture, or a character, becomes defined and limited by its contexts. Narrative requires an irreducible minimum of rationality which inevitably tames and limits the meaning of the vaguest of images. The kind of non-intellectual and anti-rational evocation practiced by the symbolist poet is incompatible with the laws of narrative, which are as inexorable as the laws of physics, though less precisely ascertainable. Rather than divide narrative artists into symbolists and allegorists, we must come to grips in the work of each artist with the kind of interaction between illustrative, representational, and esthetic impulses characteristic of his mind and art.[36]

Allegory and Realism

Before finally gathering together the elements of a profile of Hawthorne's allegory, one of the points of the above citation should be underlined. Though this essay has been consistently based on the supposition that there is a difference between realistic and allegorical fiction, it is important to recognize that the difference is relative, a question of points at opposite extremes of a continuum upon which narrative fiction might be arranged. The nature of the difference is best seen in terms of the reading experience. Ideally the reader of a work of realistic fiction should not be distracted by the desire to play with conceptual meanings until after the whole fictional structure is in view. The *meaning* of a piece of realistic fiction is its structure, the unity given to concrete realities, well-rounded and developing characters, and plausible narrative events. The abstractive and interpretative instinct must be held off as much as possible until the whole fictional unit is grasped in that single irreducible intuition which is Susanne Langer's basic insight into the nature of an esthetic experience.[37]

But if one accepts the general validity of Miss Langer's irreducible intuition as the norm for esthetic experience, it would seem that the experience elicited by the allegorist can not properly be termed esthetic. It is of the essence of the experience of allegory that from the beginning the mind is teased into making relationships between the concrete facts of the fiction and its potential abstract meanings. One may be tentative and puzzled about these abstractions, remain so throughout, perhaps never become completely sure of how they belong together in a system, but confused or not, the essence of the experience of allegory is the dialectic between the fictional facts and the conceptualizations which they suggest. Is allegory, then, merely didactic, or can the concept of irreducible intuition be broadened enough to include an experience in which the reader plays throughout with conceptual interpretation?

The answer to the question lies in the affirmation that idea-haunted as it may be allegory is still basically a way of telling a story. It may so be governed by concepts that a conceptual paraphrase is possible or it may be tentative, an ambiguous testing of concepts. But it is, more fundamentally than all this, a story, one told in such a way that its formal characteristics—the way it is told—draw the reader into playing with and assigning conceptual meanings as he goes. As Daniel Hoffman says:

> The imaginations of Hawthorne and Melville were both committed to allegorical premises and skeptical of allegorical truths. Allegory was designed for the elucidation of certainty; they used it in the service of search and skepticism, and, at times, of comedic affirmation of human values.[38]

This is an esthetic pursuit, though it has its didactic dimensions. The irreducible intuition is the perception of and the enjoyment of the conceptual byplay which goes on in terms of the story, and the ultimate realization that, as in all art, it is not the conceptual conclusion which counts, but the enjoyment of a journey of the mind and imagination.

If the interpretative struggles of these chapters have any validity, it is clear that Hawthorne is not what Northrop Frye calls an intermittent allegorist, who writes "in a *freistimmige* style in which allegory may be picked up and dropped again at pleasure."[39] Hawthorne wrote sustained allegorical narratives. Allegory so informs his fictional structures as to make it impossible to say that he ever drops or picks it up. Hawthorne differs from Dante, Spenser, Tasso, and Bunyan, not because he engages the form more loosely, but because a new phase of Western culture had broken down their world of shared cultural values, changed the relationship between artist and society, and made it necessary to reformulate the allegorical mode. In Hawthorne's reformulation allegory is made into a testing ground for the constantly changing values of the modern world.

Profile of Hawthorne's Allegory

What, then, are the characteristics of Hawthorne's reformulated allegory? First of all with reference to the reality of his fictional surface, Hawthorne falls somewhere between the eighteenth century allegorist's effort to make the surface fiction mimetically consistent and the neo-romantic's concern to alert the reader to allegory by violating the mimetic surface, giving it instead the unreal surface of dream or ritual.[40] Hawthorne cultivates an ambiguous surface reality, placing his stories in actual historical times, but violating their mimetic consistency in favor of the non-mimetic techniques of allegory. There has been some difficulty in accepting Hawthorne's departures from mimetic reality. It is stated cogently in Rudolph VonAbele's comparison of Hawthorne and Kafka.[41] According to VonAbele, we can accept Kafka's departures from realism because Kafka gives an unequivocal ontological status to his symbols, makes us accept their reality, whereas Hawthorne constantly calls the reality of his symbols into question. In the wake of science, which has emptied symbols of their reality, literature must fight to make us accept their reality before analyzing their meaning. This requirement presupposes, it seems to me, that the experience of reading a realistic novel is the normative experience. VonAbele gives his realist bias away in an earlier passage in which he states the question behind his investigation of Hawthorne:

> What follows is an attempt to answer, among others, the question that has proved most perplexing to me from the beginning: why did Hawthorne never in his formal work capitalize upon the opulence of naturalist description that he put into his notebooks? Why did he never capitalize as an artist upon the life he led among men in his various customhouse and consular positions?[42]

The answer to the question, it seems to me, is that he did use all these things, but in a literary form whose primary esthetic function was not to resist the depradations of science, but precisely to play with reality and meaning on his own, not our terms.

Hawthorne's most frequent technique of breaking the narrative surface is, of course, the interpolation of long historical essays. He employs a very effective refinement on this technique in "Legends of the Province House" and in *The Scarlet Letter*. Rather than overt, essay-like excursions into the past, Hawthorne uses realistic links with the past to step off the distance, thereby creating a sense which is exact both in terms of history and of emotion of distance and proximity, or pastness and of survival into the present. In "Legends of the Province House" the links are the house itself, whose duration is marked by the scars of change in its interior, and the ancient narrator in whose persona the tales are told. But "The Custom-House" is the master stroke of this technique. The strong sense of contemporary decay and the evocation through the letter of the once vital Puritan world is intensified by his own feeling of inherited guilt. Not his guilt, alone, however. By means of his wedding of history and allegory, Hawthorne involves us all in a public examination of our national conscience while probing tentatively for truths of universal human significance.

Though Hawthorne did not limit his examination to the Puritan period of our history, the special appropriateness of that world to his allegorical speculations is undeniable. The world of the Puritans was so haunted by a superstitious belief in unreal or preternatural forces as to furnish Hawthorne with an ideal milieu for the exploitation of the non-mimetic techniques of allegory. Within an allegorical world whose reality is so ambiguous, the principle of causality is necessarily ambiguous—Hawthorne's well-known multiple choice. In "My Kinsman, Major Molineux" dark but essentially plausible psychological causes are at work beneath the fantastic surface. Within a context with no definable boundaries between reality and dream, "Young Goodman Brown" wavers uncertainly between human psychology and a threatening supernatural world. In "The Maypole of Merry Mount" and "The Gray Champion," the stronger historical force wins, but for different reasons. In "The Maypole of Merry Mount," Endicott wins by the simple superiority of force of arms. In "The Gray Champion," however, some other force is at work:

> But whether the oppressor were overawed by the Gray Champion's look, or perceived his peril in the threatening attitude of the people, it is certain that he gave back. . . . (865)

The Gray Champion himself is unambiguously supernatural; and though Hawthorne gives us the option of ascribing the British retreat to fear of the mob, he inspires us, as well, with a sense of symbolic and supernatural causality. In "Howe's Masquerade" the causal principle is an overriding historical determinism. As Howe watches the allegorical figure of himself, we realize that he is, in Hawthorne's view, fated to make exactly the same futile gesture as his allegorical counterpart. Finally, in "Lady Eleanore's Mantle," Hawthorne gives his causal principle a religious aura by invoking Providence and by suggesting the causality of sacramental symbols. In *The Scarlet Letter* Hawthorne continues to give his causal principle the same religious ambiguity he gives the whole fictional surface. Most of the characters are what they are because of plausible psychological causes. But he plays intermittently with the notion of diabolical possession. The eschatological vision of the letter in the sky is first scoffed at as the diseased vision of Dimmesdale and then verified by the reporting of the people. Pearl's transformation from allegorical to real, though mimetically implausible, is allegorically right. Hawthorne's causal principle seems most frequently to be based on the mystery of human psychology, but especially when he moves into the sphere of society and nature he toys with a concept of causality which wavers between superstition and the providence of God. As we have seen, the Puritan view of Providence is very close to superstition.

A second technique of Hawthorne's allegory is the basic element in Northrop Frye's descriptive definition of allegory.

We have actual allegory when a poet explicitly indicates the relationship of his images to examples and precepts, and so tries to indicate how a commentary on him should proceed.[43]

Hawthorne frequently breaks through the fictional surface to give explicit interpretations of his symbols. He tells us what the red and black mean on the face of the rebel leader in "My Kinsman, Major Molineux." He plays on the conceptual meaning of the name of young Goodman Brown's wife. He calls the pillory the Puritan Maypole. He brings the confrontation of colonists and British troops to a halt to interpret the whole scene, and he concludes his tale with an interpretation of the Gray Champion himself. Among many explicit interpretations in "Lady Eleanore's Mantle," Hawthorne creates a similar static tableau at the beginning of the story and interprets both the lady and her adorer. The whole of *The Scarlet Letter* is, of course, a series of reflections on the meaning of the titular symbol. The story begins with a chapter that is static and symbolic, setting up the conflict between society and nature with an interpretation of the prison door and the rosebush.

The historical essay and the explicit interpretation of symbols both combine with the unreal fictional surface to perform a very important function which is particular to Hawthorne's restructuring of the allegorical form. Together these techniques keep the reader aware of the presence of the author and of the fact that the fictional world with which they are engaged is not theirs to enter but Hawthorne's to stand outside of and contemplate. The detachment here is not an emotional detachment; the bond of feeling between present and past is essential. But Hawthorne is not interested in indulging either nostalgia or mindless guilt. The emotion is to be meaning-centered even if it escapes ultimate rational analysis.

Hawthorne's allegory is thus more personal and more objective than the allegories of Spenser, Bunyan, and the others. It is more personal because it is self-consciously proposed as his own unique offering to a world which may or may not accept Hawthorne or the whole literary enterprise. It is by the same token more objective because no attempt is made to seduce the reader into accepting either the fictional world or any of its values as his own. He is left free, precisely because he is always confronted with the creator, to accept or reject his creation.

The above techniques account for the metaphysics of Hawthorne's allegorical world. We go on now to its cosmology and psychology: structure and characterization. In both "My Kinsman, Major Molineux" and "Young Goodman Brown" the basic structure is a series of discrete encounters between the hero and representatives of the society into which he is entering. In "The Maypole of Merry Mount" and "The Gray Champion," on the other hand, the structure is the elaboration of a stand-off between opposing social systems. We have identified these two structural patterns as the typical ones of allegory: ritual progress and battle. They are combined in "Howe's Masquerade." In *The Scarlet Letter* they exist as microstructures rather than as structural principles of the whole. Ritual processions are recurrently employed to give a sense of Puritan society, and dialectical conversations and symbolic pairs set up the opposition between the forces of society and nature.[44]

One of the techniques which is basic to the creation of a sense of the social worlds involved in these allegorical structures is decorative imagery. Ornamentation is the essential way by which the social order and its hierarchy is made visible. However, decorative imagery not only constructs hierarchy, but implies a value judgment as well. In "The Maypole of Merry Mount" the costumes of both the devotees of the Maypole and of the Puritans denigrate the hierarchy that exists among them. The colonists of Merry Mount have overturned the law of nature; the Puritans have dehumanized themselves. Involved here is a sense of natural hierarchy. When it comes to social hierarchy, however, Hawthorne takes a direction which is particular to himself. It is a paradoxical direction for an allegorist. Though hierarchy may be the very stuff of allegory, for Hawthorne social hierarchy is almost of its essence evil. Consequently he uses the allegorical technique of ornamentation not just to create social hierarchies, but also and especially to undercut them. In "The Gray Champion" the British social order, it is suggested, is a mere mask over basic disorder. In "Howe's Masquerade" a new social order of history—which favors the emerging democracy of the colonies—imposes itself and wins out over the hierarchy of rank. Finally, in "Lady Eleanore's Mantle" the whole notion of an aristocratic order is connected with pride and condemned to destruction.

The most interesting of Hawthorne's structural techniques is the use of multiple levels. These are not the multiple levels of interpretation familiar to us in the famous four senses of Medieval scripture exegesis, nor the levels of interpretation, such as religious and political, appropriate to Spenser. Hawthorne's allegories are, rather, allegories within allegories. We feel, for instance, that the devotees of the Maypole live out their own allegory within the larger allegory, created by Hawthorne, which brings them into a confrontation with the Puritans. The masquerade ball given by Sir William Howe is itself an allegory. Its already chaotic surface is shattered, however, by another allegory, the solemn procession of past governors of the colony. The ultimate allegory, however, is neither of these, but the essentially verbal battle between Howe and Colonel Joliffe, with his allegorical commentary on the subordinate allegory of the procession. *The Scarlet Letter* is the climactic realization of Hawthorne's skill at multi-level allegory. The story proper takes its beginning within the allegorical world of the Puritan crowd. But Hawthorne skilfully draws us beyond the limits of that world to his own larger allegorical perspective. The measure of his skill is his capacity to maintain an allegorical perspective as that larger historical perspective dawns upon us, so that we can see, within an allegory, the destructive potentialities of the lived allegory of Puritanism. Here again it is allegory against allegory.

Characterization raises the crucial question for those whose definition of allegory requires the personification of abstractions. If Hawthorne is the creator of fictions which are not just intermittently allegorical but structured as allegories throughout, why aren't his characters personifications of abstract qualities?

Many of them, of course, are. There is Faith of "Young Goodman Brown." Lady Eleanore and Jervase Helwyse are antithetic symbols of aristocratic pride and abject common humanity respectively. The Gray Champion is the "type" of the Puritan spirit of independence. Hawthorne also employs the traditional allegorical figure of the guide. In "My Kinsman, Major Molineux" and "Young Goodman Brown" this figure is the personification of that aspect of the hero's personality which will eventually win out. In "Howe's Masquerade" and "Lady Eleanore's Mantle" the guides, Colonel Joliffe and Dr. Clarke, are the human embodiments of the historical force that will win out in each of these stories: Colonel Joliffe is a figure of independence and Dr. Clarke a figure of the rational and the humane.

But Hawthorne has made allegory into a kind of superior realism. His characters are not simply abstractions but demonstrations of the fact that distortions of the personality are real, that men can become monodimensional, walking symbols of the diseases that infect human existence. Once more *The Scarlet Letter* is our supreme fictional example. In this novel Hawthorne recreated the lived allegory of Puritanism by peopling it with many mere personifications of functions within Puritan society. But since his thematic drive was to reveal the inhumanity of that

Puritan world, he had to create contrasting characters who at least seemed to have escaped the stereotypes of Puritan existence, to have the roundness of real people. His solution to this problem was to place within the story itself the event in which each of his central characters suffered the loss of human fullness and became monodimensional, and hence meaning-bearing personages. Hester's pain, which becomes real to us when we are allowed to share her memories of childhood, is the experience of a real person whose punishment is to have her reality constricted into a symbolic figure. Chillingworth, at his first appearance, chooses the distortion that will destroy his humanity. Pearl is brought up by her mother in the role of allegorical representative of sin, but she undergoes, at the public confession of her father, the opposite transformation into true personality. Dimmesdale hovers constantly between the symbolic role of saint and the actual role of sinner. His meaning is his ambiguity. Characterization, then, in Hawthorne's greatest allegory, is necessarily monodimensional; but it is rooted in the deeper realism of human psychology.

The interesting thing is that except in a few instances we do not feel that Hawthorne has to compensate for the reduced stature of his characters. The compensation is there already in the fact that any idea which comes under examination in his allegories is never left in its Platonic simplicity. In "My Kinsman, Major Molineux," for instance, we see both sides of the struggle for independence, and we experience the ambivalence of the strugglers. "Legends of the Province House" consists of three stories told from the point of view of the colonists but concludes with "Old Esther Dudley," a moving and sympathetic portrayal of the loyalist. But in *The Scarlet Letter* it is the depth of character revealed in its very constriction that compensates for their allegorization. Here Hawthorne penetrates far deeper than the polarities of political loyalty, and reaches out to problems well beyond the limits of the American experience alone. Hawthorne in *The Scarlet Letter* is an early prophetic voice at grips with a problem which plays in virtually every important work of fiction from the nineteenth century till now. It preoccupies writers as disparate as Henry James and Andre Malraux. Its archetypal poetic statement is "Dover Beach":

Ah, love, let us be true
To one another! for the world, which seems
To lie before us like a land of dreams,
So various, so beautiful, so new,
Hath really neither joy, nor love, nor light,
Nor certitude, nor peace, nor help for pain;
And we are here as on a darkling plain
Swept with confused alarms of struggle and flight,
Where Ignorant armies clash by night.[45]

Arnold's apocalyptic vision of the breakdown of all societies has not yet conquered Hawthorne. Though he clearly portrays the failure of Puritan society, with its universal allegorical meanings, to deal with the complexity of the human heart, he remains sensible of the need for society as the context for any valid human relationship. But he can only project that need into some vague future. Having tested and refined personal love in this deeply realized allegorical adventure of the spirit, he found that it is not enough. Truth to a larger social world, to one's fellow man, is essential. But what that world can be, how it is to come, is all very doubtful. Meanwhile, more than ever faced with the apocalyptic dreams of an onrushing future, we must continue to ask how to live and love in face of it.

NOTES

[1] Mircea Eliade, *The Myth of the Eternal Return,* translated by Willard R. Trask ("Bollingen Series," 46; New York: Pantheon Books, 1954). Note, however, that much modern biblical criticism denies the simple dichotomies involved in Eliade's thesis, without denying the thesis altogether.

[2] For an extraordinarily detailed account of the development of Jewish eschatology see Sigmund Mowinckel, *He That Cometh,* translated by G. W. Anderson (New York: Abingdon Press, 1955).

[3] Some of the standard *loci* are Gal 4:22 ff.; Col 2:17; Heb 10:1.

[4] Lk 1-2.

[5] *Op. cit.*

[6] *Op. cit.*

[7] "Hawthorne's 'Bell': Historical Evolution through Symbol," *NCF* 19 (September, 1964), 126.

[8] *Ibid.,* p. 129.

[9] *Ibid.,* p. 127, n. 3.

[10] *Ibid.,* pp. 129-130.

11 *Ibid.,* p. 124.
12 *Americana Norvegica* ("Norwegian Contributions to American Studies," Vol. 1; Philadelphia: University of Pennsylvania Press, 1968), p. 110.
13 *Ibid.,* p. 115.
14 *Ibid.,* p. 118.
15 *Ibid.,* p. 127.
16 *Ibid.,* p. 128.
17 *Ibid.*
18 Brumm, *op. cit.,* p. 121.
19 *Ibid.,* p. 116.
20 Edwin Honig, *op. cit.,* pp. 57-61, shows how biblical typology is a fundamental kind of allegory.
21 Brumm, *op. cit.,* p. 118.
22 *Ibid.,* p. 125.
23 *Ibid.,* p. 123.
24 *Ibid.,* p. 131.
25 *Ibid.,* p. 137.
26 *Ibid.,* p. 139.
27 Kjørven, *op. cit.,* p. 110.
28 *Op. cit.*
29 Brumm, *op. cit.,* p. 160.
30 *Anatomy, op. cit.,* p. 90.
31 *Op. cit.,* p. 284.
32 *Op. cit.,* p. 370.
33 *Ibid.*
34 *Op. cit.,* p. 101.
35 *Op. cit.,* p. 161.
36 *Op. cit.,* pp. 106-107.
37 *Feeling and Form: A Theory of Art* (New York: Charles Scribner's Sons, 1953).
38 *Op. cit.,* p. 5.
39 *Anatomy of Criticism, op. cit.,* p. 90.
40 John Burrow made this distinction in "Allegory: the Literal Level," *op. cit.*
41 *The Death of the Artist: A Study of Hawthorne's Disintegration* (The Hague: Martinus Nijhoff, 1955), p. 18.
42 *Ibid.,* p. 2.
43 *Anatomy, op. cit.,* p. 90.
44 Arlin Turner, "Hawthorne's Methods of Using His Source Material" in *Studies for W. A. Read,* edited by Nathaniel M. Caffee and Thomas A. Kirby (Louisiana State University Press, 1940), pp. 301-312, covers more of Hawthorne's works than are treated here and in general corroborates what my sampling indicates: that the idea is uppermost at the inception, that development is by catalogue or procession and by the creation of an atmosphere of ambiguous reality. Terence Martin, "The Method of Hawthorne's Tales," *Centenary Essays,* pp. 7-30, gives more attention to Hawthorne's creation of a time "when dreams and reveries existed as a part of actual life."
45 Matthew Arnold, *Selected Poetry and Prose* (New York: Holt, Rinehart and Winston, 1953), p. 90.

Bibliography

The following bibliography contains only works cited in the book. A list of all the works actually consulted in its preparation would have been unnecessarily long.

PRIMARY TEXTS

The Complete Novels and Selected Tales of Nathaniel Hawthorne. Edited by Norman Holmes Pearson. New York: The Modern Library, 1937.

Nathaniel Hawthorne: Selected Tales and Sketches. New York: Rinehart and Company, Inc., 1950.

Nathaniel Hawthorne. *The Scarlet Letter.* Ohio State University Press, 1962.

SECONDARY MATERIAL

Abel, Darrel. "The Devil in Boston," *Philological Quarterly,* 32 (October, 1953), 366-381.

————. "Hawthorne's Dimmesdale: Fugitive from Wrath," *Nineteenth-Century Fiction,* 11 (September, 1956), 81-105.

————. "Hawthorne's Pearl: Symbol and Character," *Journal of English Literary History,* 18 (March, 1951), 50-66.

Adkins, N. F. "The Early Projected Works of Nathaniel Hawthorne," *Papers of the Bibliographical Society of America,* 39 (Second Quarter, 1945), 127-131.

Auerbach, Erich. "Figura," *Scenes from the Drama of European Literature.* Paper; New York: Meridian Books, Inc., 1959.

————. "Satire and Theme in *The Scarlet Letter,*" *Philological Quarterly,* 41 (April, 1962), 508-511.

Bewley, Marius. *The Eccentric Design: Form in the Classic American Novel.* Paper; New York: Columbia University Press, 1963.

180

————. "Hawthorne and the Deeper Psychology," *Mandrake,* Vol. 2, pp. 366-373.

Bier, Jesse. "Hawthorne on the Romance: His Prefaces Related and Examined," *Modern Philology,* 53 (August, 1955), 17-24.

Boewe, Charles and Murphey, Murray G. "Hester Prynne in History," *American Literature,* 32 (January, 1961), 202-204.

Broes, Arthur T. "Journey into Moral Darkness: 'My Kinsman, Major Molineux' as Allegory," *Nineteenth-Century Fiction,* 19 (September, 1964), 171-184.

Brownell, W. C. *American Prose Masters.* New York: Charles Scribner's Sons, 1909.

Brumm, Ursula. *American Thought and Religious Typology.* Translated by John Hoaglund. New Brunswick, New Jersey: Rutgers University Press, 1970.

Burrow, John. "Allegory: The Literal Level." Lecture given at Yale University, October 2, 1967.

Carpenter, Frederic I. "Scarlet A Minus," *College English,* 5 (January, 1944), 173-180.

Connors, Thomas E. " 'My Kinsman, Major Molineux': A Reading," *Modern Language Notes,* 74 (April, 1959), 299-302.

Cowie, Alexander. *The Rise of the American Novel.* New York: American Book Company, 1948.

Cowley, Malcolm. "Five Acts of *The Scarlet Letter*," *College English,* 19 (October, 1957), 11-16.

Crews, Frederick C. *The Sins of the Fathers: Hawthorne's Psychological Themes.* New York: Oxford University Press, 1966.

Davidson, Edward H. (ed.). *Doctor Grimshawe's Secret.* Cambridge: Harvard University Press, 1954.

————: "Hawthorne and the Pathetic Fallacy," *Journal of English and Germanic Philology,* 54 (October, 1955), 486-497.

————. *Hawthorne's Last Phase.* New Haven: Yale University Press, 1949.

De Rougement, Denis. *L'Amour et L'Occident.* Paper, "Le Monde en 10/18"; Paris: Union Generale d'Editions, n.d., original copyright, 1939.

Dhaleine, L. *Nathaniel Hawthorne, sa vie et son oeuvre.* Paris: Hachette and Cie., 1905.

Eisinger, Chester E. "Pearl and the Puritan Heritage," *College English,* 12 (March, 1951), 323-329.

Elder, Marjorie. *Nathaniel Hawthorne: Transcendental Symbolist.* Ohio University Press, 1969.

Eliade, Mircea. *The Myth of the Eternal Return.* Translated by Willard R. Trask. "Bollingen Series," Vol. 46; New York: Pantheon Books, 1954.

Faust, Bertha. *Hawthorne's Contemporary Reputation.* Philadelphia: 1939.

Feidelson, Charles, Jr. *Symbolism and American Literature.* Paper, "Phoenix Books"; Chicago: University of Chicago Press, 1953.

―――. "The Scarlet Letter," *Hawthorne Centenary Essays.* Edited by Roy Harvey Pearce. Ohio State University Press, 1964.

Fergusson, Francis. *The Idea of a Theater.* Paper; Garden City, New York: Doubleday and Company, Inc., 1953.

Fiedler, Leslie A. *Love and Death in the American Novel.* Revised edition; New York: Dell, 1966.

Fletcher, Angus. *Allegory: The Theory of a Symbolic Mode.* Ithaca, New York: Cornell University Press, 1964.

Folsom, James K. *Man's Accidents and God's Purposes: Multiplicity in Hawthorne's Fiction.* New Haven: College and University Press, 1963.

Fossum, Robert H. "Time and the Artist in 'Legends of the Province House,'" *Nineteenth-Century Fiction,* 21 (March, 1967), 337-348.

Frye, Northrop. *Anatomy of Criticism: Four Essays.* Princeton, New Jersey: Princeton University Press, 1957.

Fussell, Edwin. *Frontier: American Literature and the American West.* Princeton, New Jersey: Princeton University Press, 1965.

Gerber, John C. "Form and Content in *The Scarlet Letter,*" *New England Quarterly,* 17 (1944), 25-55.

Granger, Bruce Ingham. "Arthur Dimmesdale as Tragic Hero," *Nineteenth-Century Fiction,* 19 (September, 1964), 197-203.

Gross, Seymour L. "Hawthorne's 'Lady Eleanore's Mantle' as History," *Journal of English and Germanic Philology,* 54 (1955), 549-554.

―――. "Hawthorne's 'My Kinsman, Major Molineux': History as Moral Adventure," *Nineteenth-Century Fiction,* 12 (September, 1957), 97-109.

————. " 'Solitude, and Love, and Anguish': The Tragic Design of *The Scarlet Letter,*" *College Language Association Journal,* 3 (March, 1960), 154-165.

Gullace, Giovanni. "Péché et pécheurs dans *La Lettre Ecarlate* et *Le Faune de Marbre,*" *Etudes Anglaises,* 15 (April-June, 1962), 113-121.

Hall, Lawrence Sargent. *Hawthorne, Critic of Society.* "Yale Studies in English," Vol. 99; New Haven: Yale University Press, 1944.

Hart, Francis Russell. "The Norm of Character in the English Gothic Novel." Paper given at the English Institute, Columbia University, September 6, 1967.

Haugh, Robert F. "The Second Secret in *The Scarlet Letter,*" *College English,* 17 (February, 1956), 269-271.

Hoffman, Daniel G. *Form and Fable in American Fiction.* Paper, "Galaxy Book"; New York: Oxford University Press, 1961.

Honig, Edwin. *Dark Conceit: The Making of Allegory.* Paper, "Galaxy Book"; New York: Oxford University Press, 1966.

Hosmer, Elizabeth Ruth. "Science and Pseudo-Science in the Writing of Nathaniel Hawthorne." Urbana: 1950.

Ignatius of Loyola, The Text of the Spiritual Exercises of. Fourth edition revised; Westminster, Maryland: The Newman Bookshop, 1943.

James, Henry, Jr. *Hawthorne.* "English Men of Letters"; New York: Harper and Brothers, Publishers, 1879.

Johnson, W. Stacy. "Sin and Salvation in Hawthorne," *The Hibbert Journal,* 50 (October, 1951), 39-47.

Jordan, Gretchen Graf. "Hawthorne's 'Bell': Historical Evolution through Symbol," *Nineteenth-Century Fiction,* 19 (September, 1964), 123-139.

Kaul, A. N. *The American Vision: Actual and Ideal Society in Nineteenth-Century Fiction.* New Haven: Yale University Press, 1963.

Kimbrough, Robert. " 'The Actual and the Imaginary': Hawthorne's Concept of Art in Theory and Practice," *Transactions of the Wisconsin Academy of Science, Arts, and Letters,* 50 (1961), 277-293.

Kjorven, Johannes. "Hawthorne and the Significance of History," *Americana Norvegica: Norwegian Contributions to American*

Studies. Edited by Sigmund Skard and Henry H. Wasser. Vol. 1, pp. 110-160. Philadelphia: University of Pennsylvania Press, 1966.

Lane, Lauriat, Jr. "Allegory and Character and *The Scarlet Letter*," *Emerson Society Quarterly*, No. 25 (Fourth Quarter, 1961), 13-16.

Langer, Susanne. *Feeling and Form: A Theory of Art*. Paper; New York: Charles Scribner's Sons, 1953.

Lawrence, D. H. *Studies in Classic American Literature*. Paper; Garden City, New York: Doubleday and Company, 1955.

Leavis, Q. D. "Hawthorne as Poet," *Sewanee Review*, 59 (Spring and Summer, 1951), 179-205, 426-458. Cited in *Interpretations of American Literature*. Edited by Charles Feidelson, Jr., and Paul Brodtkorb, Jr. Paper, "Galaxy Book"; New York: Oxford University Press, 1959.

Lewis, R. W. B. "The Tactics of Sanctity: Hawthorne and James," *Hawthorne Centenary Essays*. Edited by Roy Harvey Pearce. Ohio State University Press, 1964.

Link, Franz H. *Die Erzählkunst Nathaniel Hawthornes*. Heidelberg: C. Winter, 1962.

Lowell, Robert. *The Old Glory*. New York: Farrar, Straus and Giroux, 1965.

Lundblad, Jane. *Nathaniel Hawthorne and the Tradition of Gothic Romance*. "Essays and Studies on American Language and Literature," Vol. 4; Cambridge, Massachusetts: Harvard University Press, 1946.

Lynen, John F. *The Design of the Present: Essays on Time and Form in American Literature*. New Haven: Yale University Press, 1969.

Male, Roy R., Jr. " 'From the Innermost Germ': The Organic Principle in Hawthorne's Fiction," *Journal of English Literary History*, 20 (1953), 218-236.

―――. "Hawthorne's Allegory of Guilt and Redemption," *Emerson Society Quarterly*, No. 25 (Fourth Quarter, 1961), 16-18.

―――. *Hawthorne's Tragic Vision*. Austin: University of Texas Press, 1957.

Martin, Terence. *The Instructed Vision: Scottish Common Sense Philosophy and the Origins of American Fiction*. Bloomington: Indiana University Press, 1961.

————. "The Method of Hawthorne's Tales," *Hawthorne Centenary Essays*. Edited by Roy Harvey Pearce. Ohio State University Press, 1964.

————. *Nathaniel Hawthorne*. New York: Twayne Publishers, Inc., 1965.

Martz, Louis L. *The Poetry of Meditation: A Study in English Religious Literature of the Seventeenth Century*. Paper; New Haven: Yale University Press, 1962.

Mathews, J. W. "Hawthorne and the Chain of Being," *Modern Language Quarterly*, 18 (December, 1957), 283-294.

Matthiessen, F. O. *American Renaissance: Art and Expression in the Age of Emerson and Whitman*. New York: Oxford University Press, 1941.

McPherson, Hugo. *Hawthorne as Myth-Maker*. "University of Toronto Department of English Studies and Texts," 16; University of Toronto Press, 1969.

Miller, Perry. "From Edwards to Emerson," *Errand into the Wilderness*. Paper, "Harper Torchbooks"; New York: Harper and Row, Publishers, 1964.

Morgan, Edmund S. *Visible Saints: The History of a Puritan Idea*. Paper; Ithaca, New York: Cornell University Press, 1965.

Mowinckel, Sigmund. *He That Cometh*. Translated by G. W. Anderson. New York: Abingdon Press, 1955.

Nolte, William H. "Hawthorne's Dimmesdale: A Small Man Gone Wrong," *New England Quarterly*, 38 (June, 1965), 168-186.

Notestein, Wallace. *The English People on the Eve of Colonization: 1603-1630*. Paper, "Harper Torchbooks"; New York: Harper and Row, Publishers, 1954.

Poirier, Richard. *A World Elsewhere: The Place of Style in American Literature*. New York: Oxford University Press, 1966.

Rahv, Philip. "Hawthorne in Analysis," *The New York Review of Books*, September 22, 1966, pp. 21-23.

Rovit, Earl H. "Ambiguity in Hawthorne's *Scarlet Letter*," *Archivum für Neuere Sprachen*, 198 (June, 1961), 76-88.

Sandeen, Ernest. "*The Scarlet Letter* as a Love Story," *Publications of the Modern Language Association*, 77 (September, 1962), 425-435.

Scholes, Robert, and Kellogg, Robert. *The Nature of Narrative*. New York: Oxford University Press, 1966.

Stein, William Bysshe. *Hawthorne's Faust: A Study of the Devil Archetype.* Gainesville: University of Florida Press, 1953.

Stewart, Randall. "Hawthorne and *The Faerie Queene,*" *Philological Quarterly,* 12 (1933), 196-206.

————. *Nathaniel Hawthorne: A Biography.* New Haven: Yale University Press, 1948.

Turner, H. Arlin. "Hawthorne's Literary Borrowings," *Publications of the Modern Language Association,* 51 (1936), 543-562.

————. "Hawthorne's Methods of Using His Source Material," *Studies for W. A. Read.* Edited by Nathaniel M. Caffee and Thomas A. Kirby. Louisiana State University Press, 1940. Pp. 301-312.

VonAbele, Rudolph Radama. *The Death of the Artist: A Study of Hawthorne's Disintegration.* "International Scholars Forum," Vol. 2; The Hague: Martinus Nijhoff, 1955.

Wagenknecht, Edward. *Nathaniel Hawthorne: Man and Writer.* New York: Oxford University Press, 1961.

Waggoner, Hyatt Howe. "Art and Belief," *Hawthorne Centenary Essays.* Edited by Roy Harvey Pearce. Ohio State University Press, 1964.

————. "Nathaniel Hawthorne: The Cemetery, the Prison, and the Rose," *University of Kansas City Review,* 14 (Spring, 1948), 175-190.

Walsh, Thomas F. "Dimmesdale's Election Sermon," *Emerson Society Quarterly,* No. 44 (Third Quarter, 1966), 64-66.

Warfel, Harry R. "Metaphysical Ideas in *The Scarlet Letter,*" *College English,* 24 (March, 1963), 421-425.

Warren, Austin. "Introduction," *Nathaniel Hawthorne: Representative Selections.* "American Writers Series"; New York: American Book Company, 1934.

Wellborn, Grace Pleasant. "Plant Lore and *The Scarlet Letter,*" *Southern Folklore Quarterly,* 27 (June, 1963), 160-167.

Winters, Yvor. "Maule's Curse or Hawthorne and the Problem of Allegory," *In Defense of Reason.* Third edition, paper; Denver: Alan Swallow, n.d.

Woodberry, George E. *Nathaniel Hawthorne.* Boston: Houghton Mifflin Company, 1902.